Free to Be

A handbook to
Luther's Small Catechism

by James A. Nestingen
and Gerhard O. Forde

STUDENT BOOK

AUGSBURG PUBLISHING HOUSE
Minneapolis

Free to Be

Prepared under the auspices of the Division for Life and Mission in the Congregation and the Board of Publication of the American Lutheran Church

This student book is accompanied by a teacher's guide and a student reflection book.

Graphic design by Studio West

The cover includes a photo of "The Ten Lepers," a wood carving by Arnold Flaten in Como Park Lutheran Church, St. Paul, Minn.

Photos: ALC OCMS, page 181. Fred Anderson, 10, 47. J. Bruce Baumann/ Image, 140b. Wilson C. Egbert, 77. Copyright John H. Eggers Publications and The Brooklyn Museum (J. James Tissot), 92. Rohn Engh, 4d, 7b, 15, 25a, 34a,c, 35, 63, 80, 86, 89a, 114b,c, 170, 178, 185, 204. HJM Photos, 165b, Kellner's Photo Services, 65, 163. Jean-Claude LeJeune, 40, 89b, 136. Lutheran Society for Worship, Music and the Arts (Philip Thompson, "The Resurrection") 83. Lutheran Standard, 110, 111, 116, 153b, 203. Dean Milbrath, 126. Dale Peterson, 158. RNS, 34b, 41, 107, 144. Paul M. Schrock, 28a, 114a. St. Paul Dispatch–Pioneer Press, 133. Three Lions (Otto Dix, "The Entrance into Jerusalem"), 95a. Today's English Version of the New Testament, copyright American Bible Society 1966, 95b. Wallowitch, 4a,b,c,e,f, 7a, 8, 13, 19, 23, 25b,c, 28b,c, 54, 55, 58, 59, 61, 66, 73, 74, 81, 87, 98, 101, 108a, 120, 122, 132, 133, 140a, 147, 149, 150, 153a, 165a,c,d, 167, 173, 184, 187, 190, 192, 194, 197b.

Scripture quotations are from the Revised Standard Version of the Bible, copyright 1946-71 by Division of Christian Education, National Council of Churches, and are used by permission.

Catechism quotations are from *The Small Catechism in Contemporary English,* copyright 1968 by Augsburg Publishing House, the Board of Publication of the Lutheran Church in America, and Concordia Publishing House; used by permission. Daily Prayers and excerpts from the Smalcald Articles and Augsburg Confession are from *The Book of Concord: the Confessions of the Evangelical Lutheran Church,* translated and edited by Theodore G. Tappert. Fortress Press, 1959.

6 7 8 9

Contents

"God has made a decision about you."

Chapter 1

God's Decision

THE FIRST COMMANDMENT
I am the Lord your God.
You shall have no other gods.

What does this mean for us?
We are to fear, love, and trust God
above anything else.

God has made a decision about you. He hasn't waited to find out how sincere you are, how devout or religious you might be, or how well you understand the Bible and the Catechism. He hasn't even waited to find out if you are interested or willing to take his decision seriously. He has simply decided.

He didn't decide without knowing anything about you, though. God knows you better than anyone else could—inside out, upside down, and backwards. He knows where you are strong and where you are weak; what you are most proud of and what you'd most like to hide. But that hasn't stopped him. His decision is made.

He comes straight out and says to you: "I am the Lord your God." That is his decision—to be your God. He isn't content just to be the kind of God who hangs stars in the night, who makes trees blossom in the spring and turn color in the autumn, or who once upon a time created Adam and Eve. In his love and grace, he has decided to be *your* God.

This isn't the first time he's said it, either. God first announced his decision about you when you were baptized, when you couldn't do anything besides eat, bawl, burp, and gurgle. "You," he said, as the pastor spoke your name, "are baptized in my name. I am your God."

He has said that same thing many times since then, too. Each time that you have read or heard his word, he has stood behind it, repeating his promise to you. As you have read his promise in this chapter, he has spoken to you again. He'll do it many more times in the future.

This isn't the word of some kind of blindly benevolent uncle chuckling behind the clouds, or some weepy great-grandpa in the heavens who would give anything if you'd just be a little bit more religious. This is the God who made the heavens and the earth, the God above anything that claims to be a god. This is the God who in Christ broke the grave for you; the God who has sent his Spirit to make you his own. So when he says, "I am the Lord your God," everything that is and could be is tied up in the promise.

First, his decision means life for you. He is the one who has given you your mind, body, and all your powers; who has followed up these gifts with everything else you've needed to live from day to day. Because he has promised to be your God, you can count on him for everything good, all that you need as long as you live.

But that's not all. Having decided to be your God, he takes you the way you are—with your strengths, gifts, talents, and abilities; but also with your bad habits, selfishness, pride, and whatever else you most want to hide.

When this God says, "I am the Lord your God," he is not saying, "I will be your God when you are good enough, devout or religious enough; or when you show me that you really mean business"—not any more than a doctor says, "I'll be your doctor when you are well, but don't bother me when you're sick." God has made his decision about you and he will forgive you, taking you as you are—hiding places and all.

Still there's more. He isn't going to be your God just for the time being, until you're 18, or until a better prospect comes along. When he says, "I am the Lord your God," it is not only for the time being, but for all time, now and forevermore.

There may be suffering, death, and sorrow in the meantime. You may strike it rich or spend your life trying to make ends meet in an assembly line, driving a tractor, teaching school, or looking at people's tonsils. But once he's said to you, "I am the Lord your God," you have a future without end. He is the Lord of life and the future, and he is your God. You have his word on it.

That sounds pretty good, doesn't it? Life, forgiveness, and a future given to you and to all who hear God's promise—not because of something we've done or have to do but solely because of God's decision. It's more than good—it's the word of life and freedom for you!

The two you's

But wait. No matter how great and gracious God's decision is, there are two you's in you and one of your you's isn't going to like this promise—not a bit. It is the you born in each of us at birth. Because it is the selfish you, the you who always wants its own way, it wants you to make your own decisions, take care of yourself, and have no gods too big to handle. This you is often called the old Adam because it is the rebellious nature passed on to us from Adam and Eve. It is going to die.

The other you in you is the new one that God called out at your Baptism, when he first promised to be your God. It is the you who will be what God made you to be—a believer. It lives and thrives on God's word in Christ, and it is going to be set free from the old Adam's clutches to receive the freedom God

has set aside for his people. This you, the new you, is going to live.

Does it make sense? Or is it confusing? Maybe we'd better take a closer look at these two you's to see what they're made of and what God is going to make of them.

The old Adam's favorite words are *me, myself,* and *I.* If he had to have a slogan, he'd probably choose "I'd rather do it myself." That, in effect, is what Adam and Eve said in the Garden of Eden. And that's the old Adam's trademark.

That's why the old Adam—the old you in you—doesn't like God's decision and promise, but secretly hates it and treats it like poison. Wherever and whenever God's promise is heard, the old Adam goes to work with a vengeance.

The first thing he tries to do is make God out to be a liar by raising fears and doubts. "God's promises may be for everyone

else," he says, "but not for you. Just look at the kind of person you are." Or, "You'd better do something so God knows that you are sincere about this." Soon he has us on a merry chase, either doubting that God will keep his word, or trying to find more and more things to do in order to prove how good we are.

Another trick is pride. "You have made a wonderful decision about Jesus," the old Adam says, as if God had to wait for us to decide before he could do anything. "You are such a fine Christian that God can't help but fall all over you."

Or he may argue, "What do you need a God for? You can take care of yourself. What is there you can't get if you put your mind to it? Gods are for weak people who can't help themselves."

The old Adam's idols

No matter what the trick, though, the old Adam always has the same purpose in mind. He doesn't want God to be God. So he tries to make it look as if God is a liar who doesn't know what he's doing, or he makes it appear that God is too absent minded, blind, or fickle to keep his word.

Then, to take God's place, the old Adam brings in all kinds of idols he thinks will do God's job for him. "Here's something you can respect," he says, "something that you can count on to help you get whatever it is you want."

For example, one of the old Adam's favorite idols is money. "If only you had lots of money," he'll say, "then you wouldn't have to worry about a thing. Then you could really take care of yourself. If you wanted anything, you could buy it. If you got sick, you could get the best treatment. And there wouldn't be a place in the world you couldn't go."

Then what happens? A person who loves money goes to work to get as much as possible, and dreams day and night of what it's going to be like to be rich.

When people who worship money get some, they think that they are the wisest, happiest, and best people on earth. They feel secure because of their bank accounts, imagine that everyone loves them because they have so much, and are certain that God can't help but smile on them because they put a few dollars in the offering plate or occasionally help a poor person.

9

People like that have an idol, don't they? They fear, love, and trust money more than God or anything else. They fear it, having great respect for the power of the dollar. They love it, sure that nothing could ever be more important than money. And they trust it, confident that it will take care of everything they need.

The old Adam has all kinds of other idols to offer, too. Some are the old-fashioned kind—statues that are worshiped, or the sun and moon and stars. Other idols don't look like idols at all but, like money, are very good things when they're used properly —such as an attractive appearance, sports, good marks, a hobby or job. When they take hold of people's hearts, claiming their fear, love, and trust, they become idols just like the statues.

People can be their own idols, too. That's the old Adam's favorite. He thinks he can do it all alone, all by himself. So he goes to work to make people fear, love, and trust their own ability and strength, sure that they can take care of themselves and get whatever they need. As this happens, we strut and preen, taking God for a liar while pretending that there's nothing in the world we can't do.

That's how the old Adam operates. He always wants to take care of himself. He is the old you in each of us—the you who wants to get along without God.

That's why God has decided to put the old Adam to death. God won't be mocked or treated like a liar. He's not going to have his creation turned into a chaos, either. He has sentenced the old Adam, with all of his idols, to death.

But that's not all. God has called out the new you in you, another you who will be what he intends you to be. That's why he has given you his word that he will be your God—to make you his, to make you what he wants you to be, a person who will fear, love, and trust him above all things, a believer.

Are you starting to get the picture? In the next section, we're going to take it a little bit further and see how God goes to work to keep the old Adam in line. More than that, we'll see what he's doing to give life, hope, joy, and freedom to the new you.

Making the New You

Some teachers—maybe you've had one like this—give huge assignments and then sit back, waiting for you to do all the work. If you come with a question, they are too busy, give the impression that they think you're stupid, or get annoyed about being bothered with such problems. All that matters to them is that you finish the work on time.

Other teachers take a completely different approach. They, too, might give some good-sized assignments. But they are more than willing to help you. They give suggestions freely, help solve difficult problems, give you ideas you can use, and are willing to spend long hours with you to make sure you understand what you are doing.

That is how God helps us. When he promises to be our God, he also gives us a huge assignment. He calls us to faith, commanding us to take him at his word. But he doesn't leave us to work it out alone, yelling at us from the heavens that we'd better make new people out of ourselves and be quick about it. He stays with us, rolls up his sleeves, and goes to work to help us in every way.

God goes much further than even the best teacher, though. He doesn't just help us with our assignment—he actually does the assignment for us, going to work to give us what he commands.

He makes new people out of us himself, calling out a new you in each one of us—a you who fears, loves, and trusts him above all things.

Taking you by the ears

How? How does God give us faith? Through the ears! It comes, as Paul says in Romans 10:17, by hearing: "So faith comes from what is heard, and what is heard comes by the preaching of Christ." God goes to work to make the new you in each of us, to give us faith, by telling us of Jesus. He gives you the faith to believe that his promise is for you by speaking his promises to you.

He doesn't just say it once, either. He says "I am the Lord your God" over and over again, in many different ways. He said it to you for the first time when you were baptized. He has said it again and again since then through your mom or dad, your grandparents or godparents, through your pastors, Sunday school teachers, or possibly through some friends who have told you the story of Jesus. God will keep on saying it, too, filling your ears with the promise, to assure you and reassure you that he is your God in Christ.

But what is faith? Luther's explanation of the First Commandment uses three words to describe it: fear, love, and trust. "We are to fear, love, and trust God above all things."

The word *fear* here doesn't mean a weak-kneed, scared-of-the-dark kind of fear, but the deepest kind of reverence and the highest kind of respect. It is the kind of feeling you might get from meeting the president of the United States or the queen of England, only multiplied by as many times as God is greater than either one of them.

God gives us this kind of fear of him not by appearing before us and rippling a cosmic set of muscles, or by dangling a miracle or two from the heavens to make us ooh and ahh, but by telling us who he is, by speaking to us of Jesus. "I am the Lord your God, who brought you out of the land of Egypt," he said to Moses and the people of Israel. "I am the resurrection and the life; he who believes in me, though he die, yet shall he live," Jesus said (John 11:25). Hearing words like these—telling us who God is and what he does—gives us reverence and respect for him.

12

The second word the Catechism uses to describe faith is *love*. It is a feeling, a deep kind of affection and appreciation for all God does. But it is more than a feeling. It is the deepest sort of loyalty, the kind of loyalty that makes us say, "This one and no other"—*this* father, *my* father, *this* mother, *my* mother, or *this* family, *my* family, or *this* girl or *this* boy—"is more important than any other and I will give everything I have for him."

God doesn't dress up in his best clothes and come to the door to ask us out, or walk by in a nice dress and fresh perfume to make us sigh and fill our hearts with mush. But he gives us ears to hear the word, gives us every gift imaginable, and comes seeking us in Christ. It is his word, the word of his decision for us in Christ, that gives us love for him—the kind of love that says, "I don't want any other God."

The third word is *trust*. This is a word the hard-nosed teachers and commanders with all their bumper stickers and slogans like so well—"you've got to trust Jesus." God says, "trust me," but he doesn't stop with slogans and commands. He gives us his word that he will give us everything good, forgive us, and finally raise us from the dead. Hearing this word, the word of his promise, we can count on him for all that we need. He doesn't lie.

"He said it the first time when you were baptized."

This is the new you God is making with his word—a you who will fear, love, and trust him above all things—a believer. God works like a lover. When a man wants a woman to love him, he doesn't try to make her love him with commands—"You'd better love me or else." That would never work. Instead, he woos her by letting her know who he is, by what he says and does for her. A woman who loves a man does the same thing.

That's what God does, too. When he goes to work to make us his new people, he doesn't try to force us to love him with commands. Rather, he lets us know who he is, what he has done, and what he will do. That's what his promise is about.

Commands for the Old Adam

Why does God bother to give us commandments at all if he's going to make the new you in each of us with his promises? It's because of that other you again, the old Adam.

The first purpose of the commandments is to keep the world ready for the promise. In this way, they are like the rules in your classrooms in school. If it weren't for some basic rules, school rooms would be a chaos. Everyone would do what he or she wanted to do—coming to class and leaving at any time, talking, wandering around, fighting for the best seats, and generally raising a rumpus. Though it might be fun for a while, soon there would be no teaching or studying. So teachers make rules to keep order: "Don't talk," "take your seat when the bell rings," and so on. The rules keep the classroom in order so that the teachers can teach and you can study.

The commandments work the same way. The old Adam knows only one rule—"Every man for himself and the winner take all." When he gets loose with his idols, God isn't the only one who is mocked—nobody is safe. The old Adam will take everything he can from his neighbors and rob the earth blind. If God didn't keep the old you in each of us in order, the world would be even more of a mess than it is—filled with rebellion, contempt, murder, rape, and lies.

So, just as a teacher makes rules to keep a classroom in order for teaching, God makes commandments to keep the world in order for his promises. He uses them to pen up the old Adam, to put him on a leash so that he can't get loose and bite and devour everything in sight. In this way, God protects us and what is ours from the old Adam in our neighbors and ourselves. At the same time, he works to see to it that we all have opportunities to hear his promises.

The second purpose God has in mind for the commandments is to drive us to his promise. Here, too, they work like a teacher. Once rules have been made to keep the classroom in order, the teacher goes to work to teach and make sure that you learn your lessons—giving assignments, passing out tests, marking papers and so on. In these ways, the teacher drives you to study.

The commandments do the same thing. They don't give marks, for sure, or come to look over your shoulder as a teacher might. But they do show you how and where you are wrong. Hearing this commandment, for instance, you might say, "I guess I do have an idol—how I look or what others think of me is really more important to me than God's promises. How in the world can I ever keep this commandment?"

It may seem strange, but when this happens the commandments are doing their second job. Because the old Adam in you won't take God at his word, God haunts you with commandments. He uses them to drive you to the promise just as a farmer uses a stick to drive cattle to the barn. The commandments are meant to convince you that you can't make it alone—that you, and all of us, need God's promise in Christ. Watching the

commandments work in this way, Luther called them a "whip" or a "goad" that drives us to Christ.

The old Adam doesn't give up easily, though. He can be very tricky. Once he sees the commandments hot on his trail, he goes underground to try one last, desperate gamble—he tries to trade the commandments for the promise.

That's how commands and promises are usually put together. When you do the command, you get the promise. At home, for instance, your mother might say, "When you do the dishes (the command) you can watch television (the promise)." Or at school, "When you have taken the required courses (command), you can take what you want (promise)." That's the way the world does its business.

That's what makes the old Adam's trick so sneaky. Once the commandments have got him boxed in so that he can't get away with obvious crimes, the old Adam tries to make it look as if you can do business with God as you do with everyone else. "You get what you pay for," he says. "You give God a little of what he wants and he gives you a whole lot of what you want." Or, worse yet, "God has made a decision about you so now you have to make a decision about him."

It sounds so reasonable. But it's just one more of the old Adam's tricks. In fact, it's nothing more than the old Adam's religion. He's trying to make God look like a liar again—treating him like some cheapskate who will do anything if you will just give him a dollar.

God won't be mocked. If you try to trade with him, he may let you try it, but then he'll do to you what Jesus did to the rich young man who tried to trade with him—he'll take the best you've got and still ask for more, beating you to pieces in the bargain.

"Good Teacher," the man said to Jesus, "what must I do to inherit eternal life?" (Mark 10:17). He had the idea that Jesus would trade with him—that there was a little something he could do in exchange for God's promise. Jesus dealt with him gently at first, but when the man pressed him for a price, Jesus zeroed in on what mattered most to the man—the man's idol, his money. "You lack one thing;" Jesus said, "go, sell what you have, and give to the poor, and you will have treasure in heaven; and come, follow me" (Mark 10:21). When he heard that, the man "went away sorrowful," beaten at his own game. The man tried to buy what Jesus insists on giving as a gift.

God's promises aren't for sale—no matter how high the offer. He's not going to trade with the old Adam—he's going to put the old Adam in each of us to death.

So, just as schoolroom rules can keep order but can't teach lessons, God's commandments can keep order in the creation but they can't take the place of his promise. And just as a teacher can try to drive you to study but can't force you to learn, God's commandments can make you look for his promise but they can't give you faith. Only God can do that, and he does so with his promises, giving faith as his gift.

The whole sum

That's the First Commandment. Luther once called it the whole sum of the law and whole sum of the gospel. It sums up all the laws and commands of God because it requires the faith of the whole person—our fear, love, and trust; our hearts, souls, minds, and strength. From this commandment, all the others follow.

At the same time, the First Commandment sums up the whole gospel because it is God's promise—the promise Paul sings of in Romans 8:31 when he asks, "If God is for us, who can be against us?" Because God is for us, Paul goes on to say, nothing "in all creation will be able to separate us from the love of God in Christ Jesus our Lord."

In fact, we could say that the First Commandment sums up the whole Catechism. The Catechism is a book of God's promises. The promises begin with this one, the most important promise of all—the one we receive in Christ's name. This promise is repeated again and again—in the Apostles' Creed, the Lord's Prayer, the sacraments and the keys and confession.

At the same time, the Catechism is the story of death and birth—the death of the old you that fights and struggles against God and your neighbor, and the birth of the new you, born in the water of Baptism. That is the new you God is making in you, the you who is a believer. As he makes you new, you will discover the kind of freedom that God gives to his people—the freedom of little children that comes with the joy and certainty of his promises.

17

Chapter 2

More than a Name

THE SECOND COMMANDMENT

You shall not take the name of the Lord your God in vain.

What does this mean for us?

We are to fear and love God so that we do not use his name superstitiously, or use it to curse, swear, lie or deceive, but call upon him in prayer, praise, and thanksgiving.

When God made his decision to be your God, the first thing he did was to tell you his name. "I am the LORD," he said, "your God." Maybe that doesn't seem like such a big deal—every pagan on the street knows God's name well enough to curse with it.

But God's name is more than just a name.

In the old West, at least according to the comic books and late show westerns, it was a custom to call a person's name his "handle." "What's the handle, pod'ner," the gunslinger says. "Billy," the other replies, "Billy the Kid."

That might seem a little odd, but "handle" isn't such a bad term for a name. Knowing your name, other people—your pastors, teachers, friends and enemies—know how to get ahold of you.

Once they have your name, they can get all kinds of other information about you, too.

The people in Bible times took names a step further, making them even better handles. As they used names, the names said something about the person's character. The name Jesus means "he will save." Jesus nicknamed two of his disciples, James and John, the Boanerges brothers—"sons of thunder." If you had met some Boanerges brothers in those days, you'd have expected them to be either very strong or else quick tempered.

That's why, in Exodus 3:13-17, Moses is so interested in knowing God's name. He wasn't just looking for a label. He wanted a handle, a name he could take hold of to call on God when he needed help, a name that would tell him what God is like.

The name God told Moses is unlike any other: "'I AM WHO I AM,' is my name," he said (Exod. 3:14). When Moses wanted to ask God for help, he could call this name. It didn't tell Moses much about what God is like, though. All "I AM" says about God is that he is, he lives, he exists.

But God told Moses a second name, as well. "Say this to the people of Israel, 'The LORD, the God of your fathers, the God of Abraham, the God of Isaac, the God of Jacob, has sent me to you'" (Exod. 3:15). It is as if God said, "If you want to find out what I'm like, look at what I've done for your fathers and what I do for you."

This second name must have rung all sorts of bells for Moses. "So that's who is in that burning bush," Moses might have said to himself, "the God who called Abraham and promised to make him the father of a great nation."

God has given us his name, too, not from burning bushes or clouded mountaintops, but in Christ. "I made known to them thy name," Jesus says as he prays for his people in John 17:26. Jesus made God's name known to us not only in what he said but in what he did, through his death and resurrection. He didn't just tell us God's name—he *did* his name to make us God's own people.

What is God's name, then? It is God, God the Father who made us. It is God, God who in Christ makes us his own. It is God, God who in the Spirit calls us and makes us what we will be. Who is our God? He is the God who raised Jesus from the dead.

Now that you know God's name, don't misuse it! That's what he is telling you with the Second Commandment. Once again, it's a problem of the two you's. The old you wants either to treat God's name with contempt or to use it to get its own way. To the new you, though, the you God is calling out for himself, knowing God's name means freedom: freedom to call on God as children call on a loving father.

Making the name nothing

God's name is taken in vain whenever it is used for nothing—which is what taking it in vain means. It is used as if God were nothing and his name good for nothing.

The most obvious way of doing this is using God's name to curse. This is so common that much of the time we aren't even aware of what is being said. It is as automatic as a transmission. "God, it's cold outside." "What in God's name does he think he's doing." "Jesus Christ, he's dumb."

When God's name is used in such a way, it becomes nothing more than a comma or an exclamation point. It is something stuffed between words to hold them apart or to give them some more emphasis—it doesn't mean anything. The name of God could hardly be treated in any cheaper way.

There are stronger ways of using God's name to curse, such

as saying "God damn you," or "damn this or that." At least when the name is used this way, the old Adam admits that God can do some damning when he wants to. But the name is still treated as nothing—nothing more than a way to let off steam.

Propping up a lie

Another way that God's name is abused is by swearing falsely. This isn't the kind of swearing we ordinarily think of, using bad words. It is using God's name to swear that we are telling the truth, in court for instance, and then telling a lie. When this happens, God's name is nothing again—just a liar's crutch to prop up falsehoods.

The same thing happens in everyday language. "In God's name, it's the truth." "I'll swear on the Bible." "Honest to God." People use God's name like this because they suspect that those they're talking to don't believe them. It's like saying, "Maybe I do lie sometimes, but when I use God's name, I'm telling the truth." The God of the promise is called upon to prop up a liar. His name, again, is nothing.

For this reason, Jesus commanded us not to swear. "Do not swear at all," he said. "Let what you say be simply 'Yes' or 'No'; anything more than this comes from evil" (Matt. 5:34, 37).

There may be times when we are required to take oaths. If you are called into court to give evidence that will help your neighbor, for instance, you may have to swear an oath. But other than that, swearing for the benefit of our neighbors, we are not to swear at all.

A third abuse of God's name mentioned in the Catechism's explanation is using it superstitiously. Here the old Adam takes God's name for magic, using it in attempts to speak with the dead or other spirits, for example. Or he takes it as a name to be thrown in like a package of instant mix to get whatever a person wants: to sink a few free throws, to pass a test without studying, to find a fast way out of trouble.

When God's name is used magically, to do tricks or to get something for nothing, it is nothing again—nothing more than a magic word to be thrown around for the old Adam's benefit.

The old Adam knows how to use God's name religiously, too. If he doesn't dare to abuse it some other way, he'll teach you to use God's name to show how religious you are. When God's name is used to impress others or when we use it trying to prove to God that we deserve his gifts, we are really saying that his name, word and promise mean nothing to us. In these ways, God's name is taken in vain as often by religious people who never curse as it is by pagans who use his name to clear their throats.

Behind all of these abuses of God's name stands the old Adam's refusal to take God at his word. When God's decision to be our God doesn't matter, his name doesn't count for much either. It can be taken in vain or ignored completely, good for nothing.

Freedom in the name

But now look at it again. Knowing God's name, you know the name of the one who created everything that is and will be, the name of the one who shattered the grave, the name of the one who is opening up the future to make all things new.

To know this name, God's own proper name, is a great gift. First of all, because he has promised to be your God and told you his name, you can call to God and be sure that he will hear and answer.

When God gives his name, he doesn't leave it behind the way a salesman leaves a calling card: "Here's my name—call me if you ever need me." God gives us his own name because he *wants* us to call on him, and regularly. In fact, out of his deep love and grace, he *commands* us to pray, demanding that we use his name to call on him for all that we need.

It is a friendly command, like hearing your parents, pastor or one of your friends say, "Look, I want to help you. Name what you need and I'll do all I can." Hearing such a command, we can pray, sure that God will hear our prayers. That's the first way God wants us to use his name.

Knowing God's name, secondly, you can praise him. That's what you do when you receive a great gift. Because the gift is so great and because of the love that shows through it, you praise the one who gave it to you.

Praising God works the same way. It is not putting on a show, trying to work up enough goosebumps to impress yourself or someone else with how much you love God. Praise is what happens as God makes the new you, as he takes hold of you in the promise to make you one of his own. His word and promise open your lips in praise.

Finally, knowing God's name, you know whom to thank for all the gifts you receive. That's something else that happens as you receive gifts. While you praise the gift and the one who gives it to you, you say thanks for it.

That's why God gives us both his promise and his name— to create the new you in each of us who calls upon him in prayer, praise and thanksgiving.

God doesn't give his name lightly. It is his personal and proper name, and it is as precious to him as your good name is to you. So this is the only commandment with a threat tied to it. As God gave the commandment to Moses, it reads: "You shall not take the name of the Lord your God in vain; for the Lord will not hold him guiltless who takes his name in vain" (Exod. 20:7).

God attaches such a terrible threat because the old Adam is always trying to make his name nothing—using it to curse, to prop up lies, to put on a show of sham religion, as magic, and in other ways. But while he threatens the old Adam in you, God is at work to make you new, giving you his word and telling you his name again and again so that you can call to him confidently and joyfully. There is freedom in his name—the freedom of the promise, given as his gift.

Chapter 3

The Last Word

THE THIRD COMMANDMENT
Remember the Sabbath day, to keep it holy.

What does this mean for us?

We are to fear and love God so that we do not neglect his Word and the preaching of it, but regard it as holy and gladly hear and learn it.

From the moment you are called out of bed in the morning—by your mother, father, or an alarm clock mimicking their voices—until the moment you say goodnight, your day is filled with words. They pop out at you from the toothpaste tube, stare at you from the cereal box, and send you off to school.

When you get there, words say hello, convey lessons to you from your books and teachers, and carry fun between you and your friends. Words follow you to the athletic field, supermarket, or wherever you go. They even invade your dreams. Words make your day.

Words make the world's day, too. Business, government, entertainment—everything depends on words. Words can be a nuisance sometimes, and they don't always do the job they should. But we'd be lost without them.

Hidden in this worldwide flood of words is one word that stands apart. It hits the ear and vibrates the eardrum just like any other word. But it is different. It is the word of the God of the promise.

Having decided to be your God and having given you his name, God is going to speak with you. He is going to tell you his decision and keep calling out the new you that will be his.

But that's not all—God has made a decision about the whole creation which he wants to tell you about. He is going to make

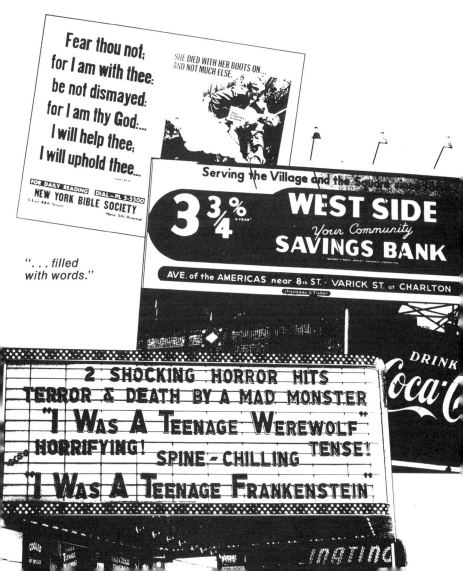

"...filled with words."

a new heaven and a new earth. Just as he had the first word at creation, he's going to have the last word, to make you and all things new.

Because it is so important for us to hear this word, God sends this commandment into all of the noise of our world. "Listen," he says, "I'm going to tell you the story of Jesus. And I'm going to tell you the end of the story, too—the end of your story and the world's story, what I've got in mind for you and my creation."

The new day coming

That is the purpose of the Third Commandment. God uses it to clear some time when he can give us his word of promise. This time also becomes a time when we can rest while we await his new day.

God's word is "living and active, sharper than any two-edged sword," as Hebrews says (4:12). It is a powerhouse, bristling, snapping, and teeming with energy and life. When God speaks, his word goes right to work.

With his word God made the world. By his word, Jesus healed the sick, drove out the demons, made the deaf hear, the mute talk, the blind see. And it's with his word, too, that God is making not only a new you but a brand new world. That's the goal he has set for everything he has made—to make all things new.

The promise of God's new creation coming is written all over the New Testament. When Jesus came out of the wilderness preaching and teaching, the promise of God's kingdom was the first word on his lips: "The time is fulfilled and the kingdom of God is at hand," he said, "repent, and believe in the gospel" (Mark 1:15).

It's this same promise that Paul sings of in 1 Corinthians 15:21-26 when he speaks of how Christ will destroy all of God's enemies—including death, the last and worst one. When that happens, the book of Revelation says, God himself will dwell with us, wiping away every tear. Then "death shall be no more, neither shall there be mourning nor crying any more, for the former things have passed away" (Revelation 21:4).

That's what God has in mind for his whole creation. Now the

old Adam is hard at work in you, struggling to strangle the new you and to be done with God once and for all. Now death looms before you, rubbing its hands together saying, "Someday, I'm going to get you." Now the creation is filled with animosity and trouble.

But that's not the end of the story. It's not going to go on like this, one day after another, everything the same. God has decided that it won't. He's going to have the last word. He's going to write the end of the story.

When God speaks that word to bring in his new day, everything—you and the whole creation—will be made entirely new. Then all of God's enemies will be destroyed. There will be no more old Adam in you to fight and struggle against the new you God has made. There will be no more death and dying to leer and grin at us, threatening and trying to destroy the creation. Anything that tries to come between God and us will be destroyed.

That's how the story's going to end—not with the cold silence of the grave but with the joy of God making all things new. Then we will have the final rest, the greatest rest of all, resting safe and secure with our Father. That's what we're looking forward to—the last word, the new day God has promised.

Resting in the word

It's because he wants to give us this word—the word of what he has done and the word of what he's going to do in Christ—that God commands us to remember the Sabbath day.

The Sabbath is like a rest stop on a long journey. If you've been on a journey or heard about somebody else's travels, you know what rest stops are like. Sometimes they are quick, with just a few minutes to fill the tank and use the facilities. But there are longer rest stops, too—better ones where you can really rest. Then you can take some time to talk over where you've been and where you're going. And you get a chance to stretch your muscles, to rest and relax before hitting the road again.

Just as you might take time from your travels to talk over where you've been and where you're going, God takes time on the Sabbath to tell us what he's done and what our destination is going to be. He tells us of the decision he's made for us in Christ—of his promise to be our God, to put the old Adam in us to death and make us new. And he tells us of our destination, of how he is going before us into the future to destroy all of his enemies and make the whole creation new.

The most important thing about the Sabbath, then, is that it is a day to hear God's word. It's not just hearing some words about God—it is God's own word, God himself speaking to us.

Maybe that's kind of surprising. In fact, you might even think it's preposterous—the very idea that Almighty God, the maker of heaven and earth, the one who raised Jesus from the dead, would ever speak to us! But it's not just an idea—it is Christ's own promise. "Where two or three are gathered in my name, there am I in the midst of them," Jesus said (Matthew 18:20). "My sheep hear my voice," he said, "and I know them and they follow me" (John 10:27).

How does it happen, then? God speaks to us by making his word like one of our words—a word fit for the lips of pastors and teachers, farmers and pharmacists, assembly line workers and astronauts, the oldest great-grandparents and the smallest

children. As your pastor and others bear witness of Christ, telling you what God has done and promises to do in him, God himself is with you, speaking to you. You have Christ's word on it—that you will hear his word.

That makes Sunday an entirely different day. Gathering for worship isn't just getting together to hear some nice words about Jesus. It is gathering together with our neighbors to hear what Christ himself has to say to us, to hear his word and to receive his sacraments.

There's something else that makes Sunday different, too. Just as a traveler's rest stop provides a chance to stretch muscles and relax for awhile, the Sabbath provides one day each week to take it easy. We are not machines that can run day and night without ever stopping. We need some time to get out from under the load. So God commands us to take at least one day off each week, a day that is free from the everyday responsibilities of work, study, and other duties. It is a day of rest, rest in the word, a holiday in a holy day.

The ear and day plugger

You can bet that the old Adam isn't going to just sit still, quietly listening while God's word is spoken, though. The word is seed, sunshine, and rain for the new you and the new creation. But for the old Adam it is his death sentence and obituary all wrapped up into one. So he squirms and fights, trying to plug your ears and your days and so deprive you of the word and the rest that goes with it.

One of the most obvious ways that the old Adam goes about plugging your ears and your days is by filling them with all sorts of other things. It is an easy trick. You have lots of studies, and there are all sorts of interesting and fun things to be done. The old Adam only has to push a little bit—convincing you that there is something you really have to do or something that would really be fun—and he can rob you of your Sabbath completely.

This strategy is so successful that the old Adam usually doesn't have to get more clever. But he can when he has to. Sometimes he attacks the word with a little bit of religion. It works like this: "I read the Bible at home, when I'm alone, and I don't need the rest of that stuff." Or, "I feel so close to God in my garden," "when I'm in nature," or someplace else "that I don't need that Sunday morning business."

If that's all there is to it, doing a little something to feel close to the Almighty, there's probably no reason to break the daily routine. But that's not the way it is; God has a word for you. Doing a little something to feel close to him is just another one of the old Adam's tricks designed to close ears to the word and deprive people of the company of others who will make them stronger.

Another of the old Adam's tricks is reserved for people who do get within earshot of the word. "Just words," the old Adam sniffs, "no action. All of it is just so much boring talk."

Or he may try to make it seem that the word is meant for everyone but you. "God may be speaking to so and so over there," he says, "but it certainly doesn't apply to you." Either way, the old Adam fills your ears with so many other things that you can't hear the word.

But don't you worry: God is at work to clear time so that we can rest and hear his word. And one day, sooner than we think, he's going to call the old Adam's number once and for all, bringing in the new day, the new creation he has promised.

That will be the end of the story that began in Jesus: God's ultimate victory, the coming of his kingdom, "the glorious liberty of the children of God" (Rom. 8:21). This promise makes Sunday an entirely different day: a day of rest to hear the word, a rest stop on the way to God's new day.

Chapter 4

The Highest Office

THE FOURTH COMMANDMENT
Honor your father and your mother.

What does this mean for us?

We are to fear and love God so that we do not despise or anger our parents and others in authority, but respect, obey, love, and serve them.

God has really turned the tables, hasn't he? Instead of teasing you with rewards or bullying you with threats to make you swing a deal with him, he's come straight out and told you the whole story. In three short commandments he's told you his decision about you in Christ, his name, and the decision he's made about the whole earth. He's said, "I'm going to be your God and make you and the whole creation new."

Now, what are you going to do in the meantime? Some people, once they hear what God has decided, think there's no point in doing anything. It doesn't seem to matter what we do anyway, they say, so why not just eat, drink, and be merry until the end.

Other people say that since God is going to write the end of the story, we'd better get busy and do some really good and pious things to prove that we are religious enough to deserve what God has in mind.

That's how the old Adam reacts.

But what does God say? After giving you his word that he is your God and telling you what the end of the story is going to be, he says: "Honor your father and your mother." Then he adds a beautiful promise to this commandment: ". . . that your days may be long in the land which the Lord your God gives you" (Exodus 20:12). He doesn't leave us alone in the meantime—he goes to work to make sure that we will enjoy long and happy lives until his new day comes.

God begins where life begins for us, in our homes. There he sets parents and children apart for the highest offices in his creation, the offices of father and mother and children. Then, having protected us in our homes, God goes on with six more commandments to make sure that life and everything we need to live will be protected as long as we live.

Representatives in your house

The promise God has attached to this commandment is the tip-off to its purpose. He doesn't say "honor your father and your mother" because he wants to set up some dictators. Rather, he wants to make sure that you get a good start in life. He wants to be sure, too, that your home and community are protected and kept in order. When parents and other authorities are just and receive their proper honor, that's what happens—the old Adam is restrained and there is justice and order so that you can live a long life.

Maybe you haven't thought of "father" and "mother" as names for offices. But they are offices just as much as the offices of mayor, president, or prime minister. In fact, they are even higher offices. Parents have the highest office in the creation because through them God gives life. When he gives life, he puts parents in charge of caring for and protecting their children.

Your parents, whether you become their child through birth or adoption, received their office before you were born. God gave it to them to make sure that you would have food, clothing, a place to live, and other necessities. But that's not all. Through your parents God has been at work to make sure that you are loved, taught, trained, and given his word and promise. Through them, too, he's been at work to prepare you for the day when you will start out on your own.

Because God considers the office of father and mother so important, he has given a high office to children, too—the office of son or daughter. And just as he gives parents a big job in their offices, he gives children a great responsibility to go with theirs: children are to honor their parents. Does that sound like a fancy way of telling you to listen to your folks? It might, but it's no fooling: God has set both parents and children apart for their offices with a very special word, the word *honor*.

You've heard that word before many times. If you get straight A's, win a contest, or earn some recognition for a project, it is an honor. As we use the word, it points to someone set apart or special.

When God uses the word it means even more. To honor someone, as he says it, isn't just to tip your hat to someone or to recognize his or her special achievement, but first of all to love that person. That is where honor starts. When you love other people—your mother and father, brothers or sisters, a special friend—they become most important to you. You appreciate and enjoy them, you are willing to do whatever you can for them, and you prefer them to others.

But honoring is more than love. It includes the highest kind of respect, respect that doesn't want to argue, question, or criticize. The people you honor are the people about whom you say, "I wish I could be like him," or "if she were here, things would really be different."

A large target

You can see, then, how important God considers parents. In all creation, parents and their helpers are the only ones God commands us to honor. They are his representatives in your house. You can see, too, though, what a big job you have and what a large target the old Adam has to shoot at in your home.

The old Adam isn't just the old you in you—he's the old you in your parents, too. They're his first target. Because they have such a big job to do, the old Adam has plenty of opportunities. It is easy for him to make them grudging or impatient, nosy,

short tempered, hard to get along with at times, or stricter than they need to be.

What do you do when the old Adam causes trouble in parents? "Honor your father and your mother," the commandment answers. There are no exceptions. Maybe that sounds kind of hard. But when God commands us to honor parents, he means business.

But God knows, too, that the old Adam can take hold of this command and use it like a club, insisting that parents be honored when he's trying to get away with his tricks in them. So God has put both a safety valve and a limit on his command.

The safety valve is other authorities God provides. When parents become downright mean, intolerable, or dangerous, it is the job of other authorities to help you—authorities like your teachers, your pastor or, if necessary, police officers or judges. If a difference between you and your parents becomes so important that it requires help from others, one of these people will help. If you don't think the difference is worth talking to other authorities about, your parents' word is final.

The one limit God has set on this commandment is that he is more important than parents are. That is what Jesus is talking about in Matthew 10:37: "He who loves father or mother more than me is not worthy of me; and he who loves son or daughter more than me is not worthy of me." Your parents are God's representatives in your house, but they don't take God's place.

The old Adam doesn't only attack parents, however. He's the old you in you, too, and you probably don't need a long list of tricks to know how he operates.

One of the old Adam's favorite tricks is to close children's eyes to all that their parents have done for them, so that they begin to think their parents haven't done anything or don't care. Another is making children act as if their parents and family exist to serve them and them alone, as if they were kings and queens living in a houseful of servants.

There are any number of tricks that can be used to fool, anger, and annoy parents until finally they surrender. When this happens, it's not long before the house is filled with angry and shouting parents and equally angry children. The love, care, and protection that God promises to give through the home is then lost.

Because the old Adam attacks both ways, the Fourth Commandment is a two-way street, running both ways to control the old Adam in both your parents and yourself. Paul explains it this way in Ephesians 6:1,3: "Children," he says, "obey your parents in the Lord, for this is right." "Fathers"—and mothers—"do not provoke your children to anger, but bring them up in the discipline and instruction of the Lord."

When the commandment works both ways, both parents and children are helped and protected.

Parents' helpers

Maybe it sounds ridiculous to call the president or the prime minister one of your mother's and father's helpers. Usually we think of it the other way around—that heads of state are the really important people while parents are a drop in the bucket in comparison. But that's not the way God orders things. No matter what country or kind of government, parents come first. The other authorities are to help your parents care for you.

Though your parents can provide most of the important things you need, there are some things they can't do. Most parents lack either the time or the training to give their children a full education. While all Christians can speak God's word and promise to their neighbors and children, full-time preachers and teachers are needed in each community. Governments are needed, too, to keep order, provide for justice, and defend the citizens.

Because these authorities help your parents, they come under the protection of the Fourth Commandment as well. To do their jobs, such authorities—including teachers, principals, and pastors; government representatives, policemen, judges, and others—need the respect and allegiance of the people they are supposed to help. Without it, they can't keep order or give the help and protection they are called to give.

The old Adam, of course, attacks schools, churches, and governments with as much vengeance as he attacks parents and children. As he takes hold, these authorities may become irresponsible or power hungry. When that happens, voters have the right and the responsibility to elect new officials who will do their jobs properly.

The second table

You can begin to see, now, how far God goes to make sure that each of us is taken care of properly. He wants to make sure that we can all expect to live long and happy lives while we await his new day. So, beginning with our parents, he surrounds us with people who will help to care for us in the meantime, not only authorities but friends and neighbors.

To make sure that we can live together with friends and neighbors in peace and harmony, God has given the remaining commandments. In them, you will see how he extends his protecting hand even further, protecting all that we and our neighbors need: our lives, friendships and marriages, property, names, and the hope that we need to live each day.

These commandments, from the fourth through the tenth, are called the second table of the law. In the first table, the first three commandments, God tells us about our relationship to him. Now, in the second table, he tells us about our relationship with our neighbors, commanding us to love them in every way.

These commandments aren't going to make new people out of us. That's not their purpose. But they will protect us from the old Adam and drive us to the promise. Making the new you and the new creation is a job God won't give to anyone else— that's a job he does by himself.

Chapter 5

The Gift of Life

THE FIFTH COMMANDMENT
You shall not kill.

What does this mean for us?
We are to fear and love God so that we do not
hurt our neighbor in any way, but help him
in all his physical needs.

When car manufacturers sell cars, they usually put guarantees on them—two years or 24,000 miles, for instance, whichever comes first. Sometimes the guarantee is more, sometimes less, but once the time is up, you're on your own. If anything goes wrong, you pay the bill.

When you give a gift to someone you really care for, something different happens. You don't just give the gift and then turn your back on the person you gave it to—you want to see that person enjoy the gift. You don't turn your back on the gift, either. You make sure that it works and you see to it that no one takes it away from the person you gave it to.

That's how God gives life—not like a car manufacturer who has to worry about his profit, but like a lover who wants to take care of the one he loves and the gifts he gives. Because he's a lover, God doesn't give or do anything part way. He goes all the way to make sure that his people and the gifts he gives are protected.

That's what's behind this commandment. Having protected life where it begins with the Fourth Commandment, God now follows us out the door of our homes into our neighborhoods to protect our lives there.

He goes even further. He not only forbids killing—the actual act of taking another person's life—he forbids anything that even comes close to it. These are Jesus' words: "You have heard it said to the men of old, 'You shall not kill; and whoever kills shall be liable to the judgment.' But I say to you that every one who is angry with his brother shall be liable to the judgment; whoever insults his brother shall be liable to the council, and whoever says, 'You fool!' shall be liable to the hell of fire" (Matt. 5:21-22). These are hard words, but when the old Adam is on the loose, God's not going to take chances. He puts up not only a barbed wire fence to keep the old Adam in, but strong mesh where he tries to sneak through.

Murder and the living death

Since life is God's gift, he won't allow anyone else to take it away. That doesn't always stop the old Adam, though. When he sets his mind to killing, he can invent as many ways as he needs to get the job done. So there are many different kinds of killing.

The first and most obvious one is murder. There are many kinds of murder, too: premeditated murder, where one person deliberately sets out to kill another; passion murders, where a person kills in a fit of anger or jealousy; and manslaughter, like many car accidents, where a person is killed through carelessness.

Another kind of killing is suicide—killing yourself. Just as God forbids other people from taking your life, he forbids you to take your own. Since life is his gift to you, he wants you to keep it as long as possible.

There is still a third kind of killing—one that isn't quite as obvious. It is an indirect form of murder. It happens when people withhold help that could mean the difference between life and death. In car accidents, for instance, an injured person's life can depend on fast medical care. If people refuse to help when such help is needed, they can kill without ever raising a finger.

In the same way, when people who have plenty of food refuse to help those who are starving, they also become killers. They might not deliberately set out to kill, or even know the people who are starving, but by withholding what other people need to live, they become killers just the same.

That's the barbed wire fence—God forbids taking another person's life in any way, no matter how obvious or hidden it might be. But here's where the old Adam tries to crawl through. When

he's afraid to kill outwardly, he tries to kill inwardly—using tricks that leave his victims alive but hurt in some way. Jesus mentions three examples: becoming angry, insulting, and calling people names.

What's wrong with anger, insults, and name calling? They are just words—no one ever died of an insult. Maybe so, but words are powerful. If they don't kill directly, they stop just short of it. It can be awfully painful when someone becomes angry with you, when you are insulted, or called a name. Even if you feel the other person is unjustified, the words can strike like a club. That's why Jesus considers anger, insults, and name-calling forms of killing.

The same kind of thing can be accomplished without words, too. Refusing to speak to someone seems harmless. But only the dead don't communicate in some way, and only the dead aren't worth talking to. Refusing to speak to someone is another form of killing that causes a living death.

That's how God protects the gift of life he gives us. He forbids us to "hurt our neighbors in any way," whether outwardly or inwardly, whether openly or in secret. He is a lover, a lover who

does everything he can to protect those he loves and the gifts he gives.

God doesn't stop here, either. When he gives us life and the gifts that go with it, he puts us to work with our gifts to help our neighbors. When that happens, the old Adam takes a double beating—he not only can't inflict suffering, but he has to take a back seat while the new you goes to work to help others.

How do you help your neighbors? "With all of their physical needs," the explanation of the commandment says. Physical needs include food, clothing, shelter, and anything else that helps them maintain a full life.

Your neighbors can be helped with these needs in many ways. They are helped, for instance, through jobs your parents and you yourself do, now and in the future. God has arranged his creation so that whether we want to or not, in just about any kind of job we end up helping others. A barber or a hairdresser helps by cutting hair; a plumber helps by running pipes full of water through people's homes; a taxi driver gives rides; a farmer grows crops needed for food; a doctor finds ways to heal; a teacher helps people learn about life, and so on.

Beyond our jobs, we help our neighbors with their physical needs by keeping our eyes open for what they need. Is your neighbor hungry? Feed him. Is she sad? Encourage her. Lonely? Visit him or her.

How far does it go?

How much help should you give? Answer that by answering another question: how much help do you need? Give your neighbors as much help as you would like in the same situation.

This commandment, then, besides being a fence becomes a prod. God uses it not only to protect us against the old Adam's appetite for killing, but to drive us to Christ and our neighbors.

If the old Adam can make things tricky, as he certainly does, he can also make them complicated. Sometimes there seems to be a choice between either killing or being killed. Then there is a question: Are there some kinds of situations where it is necessary to kill?

One of these situations comes in times of war. When one country attacks another, there is killing—wholesale killing. What should Christians do? If we fight back, either by joining one of the armed services or by supporting the war, we wind up killing. If we don't fight back, both we ourselves and our neighbors—whether next door or across the country—may very well be killed.

Should we break the commandment and kill in order to protect ourselves and our neighbors? Or should we refuse to kill because God has forbidden it?

A clue in our neighbor

The first clue to answering these questions is in our neighbors. God has commanded us to help them in all of their needs. That includes protecting them when their lives are threatened. If your country is attacked, your neighbors are attacked. God wants you to help them. If you support the war or go off to fight, you aren't killing for your own benefit, but to protect your neighbors. Killing is never good, but at such times it may be necessary.

Other questions related to the Fifth Commandment can be at least as complicated as the question of war. One example is abortion—taking the life of an unborn child. Abortion is clearly wrong. The life of an unborn child does not belong to the mother or the father or to the child itself. It is God's. Taking life is killing.

There are some situations, though, where abortion might be the lesser of two evils. It can happen that bearing a child might kill the mother or result in a terrible kind of living death, causing great damage to the mother, the family, or the child itself. Then it is a question like war: no matter what happens, somebody is going to be killed or forced into terrible suffering. In this kind of a situation abortion may be the better of two extremely bad alternatives.

God not only gives life freely, but he begins to protect it before we are even born. And he follows us with his protection throughout our lives, protecting us not only from murderers and other outright killers, but from the kind of living death the old Adam also inflicts. To protect us God has surrounded us with neighbors and commanded them to help us in all of our physical needs. To protect them, he gives us the same commandment, commanding us not to hurt our neighbors in any way but to help them in every way.

Chapter 6

Saying No to Say Yes

THE SIXTH COMMANDMENT
You shall not commit adultery.

What does this mean for us?
We are to fear and love God so that in matters of
sex our words and conduct are pure and honorable,
and husband and wife love and respect each other.

This commandment has sometimes received a bad name as a
spoilsport. It is taken as a gigantic NO written over anything and
everything connected with sex, as if it were a dumptruck full of
guilt ready to drop its load on anyone caught even thinking
about it.

There *is* a no in the commandment: "You shall not." But that
isn't all there is to it. God says no to adultery—sexual relations
outside of marriage—because he wants to say a much bigger YES
to the companionship you have with your friends and to the
marriage you're likely to have someday.

The purpose of this commandment, then, is the same as the
purpose of the Fourth and Fifth: protection. As he protects the
gift of life in our homes and neighborhoods, God also wants
to protect what is nearest and dearest to life itself: friendship

and love. So God says no to adultery, to protect not only you but your whole community.

When two become one

From the beginning of the creation, God has been concerned that all people have some companions or friends—that no one is left completely alone. Next to life itself, companionship is one of his best and most important gifts. God wants to make sure that we have plenty of it while we await his new day.

If you think over your friendships, or what it's like to be without friends, you can see some of what makes them so much fun and so important. To start with, friends are people you can enjoy—people you have things in common with, people who are interesting and fun to be with. But there's more to it. A friend is someone you can confide in and trust. You can talk to your friends about what troubles or angers you, confident that they won't betray you. And when you need help, you can be pretty sure that your friends will give it to you.

It's not only a one way street, though. Part of what makes friendship so enjoyable is that your friends do the same with you, confiding in you and leaning on you for help as it's needed.

There's only one kind of companionship closer than friendship —that is marriage. "From the beginning of creation," Jesus says, " 'God made them male and female. For this reason a man shall leave his father and mother and be joined to his wife, and the two shall become one flesh.' So they are no longer two but one flesh" (Mark 10:6-8).

When a man and a woman become one flesh in marriage, it has all the marks of a friendship. They enjoy one another's company, confide in one another, and depend on one another for help. But marriage goes further than friendship—it is a man and a woman giving themselves to one another completely, as lifetime partners in God's promise.

An important part of this giving is sexual. The man and the woman become one flesh in their bodies, expressing their love for one another by giving their bodies to each other.

As they become one in their bodies, husbands and wives become like one person. Though they are still two people, they are united so that they can be together without fear or shame, shar-

45

ing all that they have—their days, months, and years; their abilities and disabilities; their gifts and needs; their whole selves.

This companionship is the first purpose of marriage. With it, God gives another gift: children. That's the second purpose of marriage. Through it, God gives life to families and new generations of people.

Marriage is both private and public. It is a private companionship, one that belongs to husbands and wives by themselves. But especially as a child or children are born, marriage is also public. The husband and wife become father and mother, taking on the offices we spoke of in the chapter on the Fourth Commandment.

Your community has an interest in marriage, too. As your parents married, they received the gift of companionship God gives with marriage. Through that gift, you received your gifts—life and all that goes with it. And now, through both your parents and you, your community receives gifts. Communities of people begin in marriages and families, receiving not only more people but the help and service each family gives.

Now there are some people who don't marry. Sometimes it is because they choose not to, believing that by not marrying they can make best use of the gifts and talents they have. Sometimes there are other reasons, such as not getting the right opportunity. Whatever the reason, God sees to it that no one is left completely alone—that all of us have companions. Unmarried people have their own special gifts to bring to our communities, too.

When two become three

When two become one in marriage, they can soon become three by having children. But they can also become three in another way—by the interference of another person from outside the marriage. That's what happens in adultery. If marriage is a circle with two halves, adultery is a triangle that breaks it.

It doesn't only happen in marriages. Sometimes two become three in friendships. Maybe that's happened to you—that you've had a close friend and lost him or her to a third person. Or maybe the third corner of the triangle hasn't been a person at all but some new interest or hobby your friend has taken up. It happens both ways and as it does, the friendship you've had is broken.

Now there's no law, in the commandments or anywhere else, that says friendships have to last forever. That's an important part of your freedom. As you change and develop new interests, you have to be free to change your friendships, too, making new acquaintances who share your interests. God doesn't limit us to one friend apiece.

But when two become three in a marriage, it's a different story. If the old Adam succeeds in making the circle a triangle, all the gifts God gives in marriage are broken. That's why the commandment against adultery comes right after the commandment against killing—it is the closest thing to murder. Though no person may be killed, in adultery a marriage dies.

Adultery kills

The first thing adultery kills in a marriage is the companionship. It's like discovering that your closest friend has been telling your secrets, only a dozen times as bad. When a man gives his body to another woman, or a woman gives her body to another man, the trust and confidence they've had with their partners are broken. They can't be sure of each other anymore, or be together without suspicion of some kind.

When the companionship between a husband and wife is broken, the children get caught too. They don't get the kind of loving care and help from their parents that God gives through families. And even if they aren't left without a father or mother, they still bear the burdens of their parents' troubles.

Finally, the community is hurt by adultery. The third person in the triangle is usually a part of the community, too, and comes from a family. Then there are two families in trouble. But even if it's just one family, adultery breaks that family's gifts and causes problems for others.

That's why God forbids adultery. The old Adam can get some satisfaction in it, crowing about having some pleasures. But that pleasure rebounds to destroy the gifts God wants all of us to receive.

That's why Jesus has tightened up this commandment, too. "You have heard that it was said, 'You shall not commit adultery.' But I say to you," Jesus said, "that every one who looks at a woman lustfully has already committed adultery with her in his heart" (Matt. 5:27). With the commandments, God puts a fence around adultery where it ends—in another person's bed. With these words, Jesus puts a fence around adultery where it begins—in the desire of the heart.

It might seem that Jesus is being too strict. Sex is exciting—it's very easy for men and women to look at one another, daydreaming about how much fun it might be to try each other out. "Just looking" doesn't seem to hurt anyone.

But that's where adultery begins—in looks and daydreams. "Just looking" isn't "just" looking, Jesus says, but adultery already. The triangle is starting to form, even if it's only in your mind.

Jesus isn't only speaking of people who are already married here. "Anyone," he says, "anyone who looks lustfully. . . ." Though you may not marry for several years, or get married at all, God is already at work to protect you and the gifts he will give if and when you do marry.

It's not that God considers sex evil or nasty and wants to blind you until your wedding day. Your sexuality and the desire that goes with it are God's gifts to you. But while he gives you these gifts, God wants to make sure that you are free to change friends as you need to. So he forbids you to give your body to anyone until you have publicly declared that it's the person you want to spend your life with. In this way, God protects your freedom now and the joy of the marriage you will probably have in the future.

For a lifetime

Jesus had some strong words to say about divorce, too. "But I say to you that every one who divorces his wife, except on grounds of unchastity, makes her an adulteress" (Matt. 5:32).

Now again, those words seem terribly strict, especially to the old Adam. The old Adam always wants to serve his own ends, and so would like to be free to do whatever pleases him.

But Christ wants to protect marriage as much as possible and to keep the old Adam in line. That's why he says this no to divorce. When you give yourself to your husband or wife, Christ wants to be sure that it is for your lifetime—that you receive all the gifts of marriage not only part time but full time.

Sometimes the old Adam will turn these words around and try to use them to his own advantage, though. In some families, the marriage may be so totally broken that divorce may be the only way to prevent further damage. In such cases, the old Adam will sometimes piously invoke Christ's words and say that divorce is impossible, just so he can do more damage. When that happens, divorce may be the best of bad alternatives.

There are some huge NO's in this commandment. God says no to adultery and anything that comes close to it. At the same time, though, he is saying a much bigger YES to you, doing everything he can to protect you and your marriage and commanding you to do the same.

God does something besides commanding and protecting, too: he forgives. When the old Adam succeeds in making a triangle—whether it is in adultery by looking, adultery in somebody else's bed, or a divorce—God doesn't come around to say, "I told you so." Instead he says, "I am the Lord your God," renews you in his promise, and keeps right on working to give you companions while you await his new day. That is a gift even greater than life and marriage: that in Christ God promises to be our God, a greater companion than anyone else could ever hope to be, forever.

Chapter 7

A Parade of Thieves

THE SEVENTH COMMANDMENT
You shall not steal.

What does this mean for us?

We are to fear and love God so that we do not take
our neighbor's money or property, or get them in
any dishonest way, but help him to improve and
protect his property and means of making a living.

What's God doing worrying about property? In each of the
other commandments he's been protecting life in one way or
another. Is property as important as life—important enough for
God to be concerned about? Why should the God of the promise bother himself about the change in your wallet, the clothes
that hang in your closet, the plate on your table, the bicycle in
your garage?

There's an easy answer: God is concerned about your property
because there are some things you can't live without while you
await his new day. Food and clothing, to start with. And that
means money to buy them. You need a place to live and medicine when you're sick. When you go to work you need books
or training, tools, some kind of transportation. Because he knows

51

that you need these things and others, God has forbidden anyone to take them from you unfairly.

But there's another reason for God's concern for property. All property belongs to him—every last shred of it. He made everything. So, while he protects your interests and your neighbors', he's going to protect what he's made, too.

It takes a thief

God has arranged his creation in such a way that all of us wind up trading with other people. Whether it is 15 cents for a candy bar, 50 cents for a loaf of bread, or $500 for a used car, it is the same basic rule: to get what you want you give somebody what he or she wants.

When this trading is done fairly, everyone benefits. Take a loaf of bread, for instance. The basic ingredients in the bread started out as wheat in a farmer's field. The farmer got some benefits by selling the wheat to a co-op or milling company. The miller, in turn, benefited by grinding the wheat into flour and selling it to a baker. The baker benefited by baking bread from the flour and selling it to a supermarket. The supermarket's owners and employees benefit by selling the bread to you. And finally, you and your family benefit by eating it.

That's the way trading is supposed to work. God has given each one of us something that our neighbors need so that by trading all of us help one another. As God gives us these gifts, he wants to be sure that they are used properly, that there is justice for all in trades that are fair and square.

The old Adam has a different idea. When God speaks his word of promise, the old Adam either turns up his nose at it or insists on trading for it. But when he sees something that belongs to our neighbor, the old Adam is all hands, ready to grab as much as he can get. All that matters to the old Adam is his own well-being. He is the old you that always wants something for nothing.

That's why God forbids stealing. In a fair trade, everyone benefits. But in stealing, only the thief profits. The neighbors are robbed of the goods they are supposed to get from what God has given them. If you can manage to get out of the supermarket with that loaf of bread without paying, for instance, you'll get the loaf of bread and save 50 cents or so. But the owner of the supermarket will take a double loss, losing both the bread and the extra money it takes to buy another loaf.

That kind of stealing—shoplifting—is easy to recognize. So are burglary and robbery, pickpocketing, purse snatching, and other open kinds of theft. But there are many other kinds of thievery which aren't so easily recognized. They don't appear to be thefts, and so they often slip by unnoticed.

One of them is dishonest trading. This happens, for instance, when merchants overprice or sell shoddy, poorly made merchandise. It is not wrong to make a reasonable profit—storekeepers deserve some benefit from what they sell. But merchants who overcharge take far more profit than can rightfully be asked, and the customers go away with less than they deserve.

The same goes for shoddy merchandise. A car dealer who sells your family a poorly made car steals several times—once when you don't get what you've paid for, a good car, and after that every time the car has to be taken back for repairs that shouldn't have been needed in the first place.

The most common theft

This kind of stealing—dishonest trading—is by far the most common form of theft. There are all kinds of people who sell their services for outrageous prices just because they can get away with it. There are all kinds of other people who don't pay for the services they receive. There is hardly an employee working who doesn't steal a few minutes from an employer when there's a chance. And there aren't many employers who lie awake nights worrying about paying their employees enough.

The parade of thieves is awfully long. At the front are burglars, robbers, shoplifters, pickpockets, and swindlers. Behind them comes a much longer line of dishonest traders and dealers. And behind them follow all of us who try to get more from our neighbors than we are willing to give in return. That makes the whole world a parade of thieves, all of us marching along as the old Adam beats his drum to convince each of us to grab as much as we can get.

"By forbidding
stealing,
God protects
each of us."

Hello There!
Please Leave all
yours Shopping bags
at the counter
We will appreciate
it very much.
Thank you
I am not for sale.

God is speaking to all of us with this commandment. By forbidding stealing, he protects each of us so that we will be able to keep what we need to live until the new day.

The Creator and his stewards

God has another reason for being concerned about property—it is all his. So he wants to make sure that it is used properly. Jesus tells a parable in Matthew 25:14-30 that shows how this happens. The parable is about a man who went on a trip.

Before he left, the man called in three of his servants and gave them some of his property to take care of. The first servant got five talents, about 75 years worth of his own wages. The second man got two talents or 30 years worth of wages. And the third servant got one talent to look after, or 15 years worth of wages.

As soon as the owner left town, the first two servants went to work. They traded with their master's money, buying and selling. By the time the master returned, they had doubled his money.

The one-talent man wasn't as brave. Maybe that isn't so surprising. Being left with even a year's worth of wages to look after would be a big responsibility. So, afraid of everything that might happen to the money, the man buried it. When the master returned, the servant dug up the talent and gave it back.

As you can imagine, the master was pleased with the first two servants. As you can imagine, too, he wasn't at all pleased with the third servant.

What do you make of this parable? First of all, look at how generous and trusting the master was. He gave each of his servants a tremendous amount of money. He didn't threaten or warn them about what would happen if they lost it. "He entrusted to them his property," Jesus says.

A second hint is how the two servants used their master's money. They helped their master by getting him a return on his money. And they helped their neighbors by trading with them.

A third hint is in what the third servant did. His talent didn't do anyone any good, neither the master nor any neighbors, nor the man himself.

Who is that generous?

Can you put the hints together? Who would ever be as generous as that master, or as trusting? Which master is concerned that we serve not only him but our neighbors?

The master in the parable is like the God of the promise, isn't he? Only God is even more generous. After he has announced his decision, "I am the Lord your God," he goes to work to give us and our neighbors everything good. He makes his sun shine and his rain fall on the good and the bad alike (Matt. 5:45).

What's more, when he gives us all of these great gifts, he doesn't look over our shoulders like some anxious father or mother, afraid we won't be able to handle his gifts. He trusts us to use the things he gives us to help our neighbors "improve and protect their property and means of making a living."

There is also a word of warning in this parable, though. God doesn't look over our shoulder to make sure we use wisely the property he gives us. But he won't be mocked, either. That's what the third servant found out.

God doesn't give us property to be kept only for ourselves. He gives it to us to be used for his benefit, the benefit of our neighbors, and finally for his own good. He won't stand for the old Adam's selfishness, greed, and hoarding.

Each day God gives us everything we need to live while we await the day when his kingdom will come. But while looking after us and our neighbors, he also looks after his own interests, not by beating us over the head, but by trusting us to use what we're given to serve him and one another.

Chapter 8

Fencing the Heart

THE EIGHTH COMMANDMENT
You shall not bear false witness against your neighbor.

What does this mean for us?
We are to fear and love God so that we do not betray, slander, or lie about our neighbor, but defend him, speak well of him, and explain his actions in the kindest way.

Do you think God knows your name? It might seem impossible. You are just one person—not only one in a million, but one in billions.

But God does know your name. In fact, when he made his decision to be your God, he gave you your name. It happened when you were baptized. As the pastor spoke the word and washed you with water, God joined your name to his. "John Peterson" or "Susan Miller," the pastor said, "I baptize you in the name of the Father, and of the Son, and of the Holy Ghost."

God not only knows your name—he is as concerned about your name as he is about his own. You remember how God protects his name with the Second Commandment. In this commandment, he is doing the same for yours. And he protects your name for the same reason: it is your handle. People use it to get ahold of you, to speak with you and about you. A good name means freedom: the freedom to live and move and serve as you await God's new day. So God protects it.

The freedom in your name

You don't have to look far to see the differences between a good name and a bad one. Classmates who have good names with your teachers, for instance, have an easier time of it. If there is any trouble in your classroom, the teacher will usually assume that those with good names aren't to blame. And when it comes time for grades, a student with a good name will usually get the benefit of the doubt—an A minus instead of a B plus. A bad name works just the opposite.

The kind of name you have makes a big difference with your classmates, too. Whatever causes it, when people get bad names

they soon learn that there are some people who won't have much to do with them. If the word gets out that they take drugs, steal, or that there's something else wrong with them, people avoid them.

The kind of name you have, then, is awfully important. It makes a tremendous difference in how well you do at school, what kind of friends you have, and the kind of opportunities you get.

The name you get now will follow you away to college or to a job, too, in your records and recommendations. And the name you get there—whether it is at a university or on a job somewhere—will follow you the rest of your life.

No wonder, then, that God is so concerned about your name. It's not only a handle—it's a key. When your name is good, there is all kinds of freedom in it: it opens doors so that you can go places and do things; people accept, respect, and appreciate you. If your name gets bad, the doors close, there are places you can't go, things you can't do, friends you can't have or keep.

There's nothing the old Adam wants more in both you and your neighbors than to build up a name that people respect.

If you can get hold of that kind of key, he can open the doors to all kinds of other tricks.

To get this kind of name the old Adam takes shortcuts, trying to make a name for you by dragging down the names of others around you.

The name dropper

One place the old Adam can do this is in law courts. When people are sued or accused of crimes, their names are at stake. If they lose, they will be fined, spend years in prison, or both. And the bad names they get will follow them for many years.

With so much at stake, the old Adam has good hunting in the courts. To drag down the name of another person there, all it takes is a few lies or half truths on the witness stand. The witness can claim a good name for testifying against a lawbreaker, and the victim pays the cost of it.

That is the first thing God forbids with this commandment: bearing false witness against someone in a courtroom or other places where authorities are searching for the truth. God forbids it not only to protect you and your neighbors, but to keep order in your community. Lying witnesses destroy the justice we need to live together peacefully.

But courtrooms are just the beginning. The old Adam can hunt names wherever people talk with one another, whether it is at school, in church or a restaurant, on the phone, or on paper. And he has a whole arsenal to hunt with. One of the old Adam's weapons is slander—saying something false about another person that damages the person's reputation. Another is betrayal—passing along someone else's secrets or other information they'd prefer to keep private. A third is gossip—truths, half truths, and rumors that put other people in a bad light.

All of these weapons are easily used. They strike quietly in little comments like "that teacher isn't fair," "that girl is stuck up," "that fellow cheats." But no matter how small they seem, these comments can do terrible damage.

In fact, whole sexes and races of people have gotten bad names from small comments. Men have taken away part of the good names of women by saying that they are less able than men. Groups that seem different, such as Blacks, Indians, Chicanos and other minorities, have lost much of their freedom because of these kinds of attacks. Once good names are lost, the freedom that goes with them is very difficult to regain.

To protect our good names and our freedom, then, God has forbidden the old Adam to use any of these weapons or to do anything else that hurts somebody's name.

God goes further, too. He commands us to care for our neighbors' names. That includes defending our neighbors when others speak ill of them, finding opportunities to say good things about them, and giving them the benefit of the doubt when they do something wrong.

To the old Adam that seems terribly unreasonable. As he sees it, other people's faults and failings are an opportunity to make you look a little bit better. "You might not be so good," he'll say, "but at least you're not as bad as that person." If he doesn't dare speak about others' faults openly, the best he can manage is to be silent about them, gloating to himself about how you'd never do such things.

But as Christ makes the new you, something different happens. Because God has given you your name and cares for you, you can see to it that other people's names are cared for, too. Then

it's not just a matter of keeping silent when others' names are attacked, but a matter of seeing to it that their names are kept open and the freedom in their names is protected.

Jesus has taken the protection of this commandment one step further by suggesting a way to handle differences that come between neighbors. Because we aren't in heaven yet, there are bound to be differences. Whatever causes them, these differences are a golden opportunity for the old Adam. To prevent him from using these opportunities for the worst, Jesus has laid out three steps to take care of the problems.

The first step is to speak to your neighbor. "If your brother sins against you," Jesus says, "go and tell him his fault, between you and him alone. If he listens to you, you have gained a brother" (Matt. 18:15). That is the last thing the old Adam wants to do. Instead, he tells the whole neighborhood or, if he's more timid, at least some strategically placed friends. If he speaks to his neighbor about it at all, it is only after he's gotten all of the mileage he can out of the fault.

Jesus turns it around. If your neighbor says or does something that bothers you, that person should be the first to know. Then he or she can explain or apologize. If what bothers you isn't important enough to take the risk of talking to the person who caused the problem, the best thing to do is to keep quiet about it.

Telling your neighbor about something that offends you doesn't automatically mean a change, however. So Jesus has suggested a second step. "But if he does not listen, take one or two others along with you" (Matt. 18:16). It is at this point that the old Adam becomes a tattletale. After blowing it all over the neighborhood when he finds some difference with his neighbor, the old Adam finds someone to tattle to—the teacher, the pastor, the police, or some other authority. If he can't get his own way he'll use the authorities to get it for him.

A second chance

But, Jesus says, give your neighbor a second chance. Take a couple of other people along with you and talk to your neighbor again. That way, the neighbor has another chance to learn that you are serious about the problem and want to have it solved. If the person still won't come around, you have the benefit of some witnesses who know that you have done everything you can to take care of the problem.

The third and final step is to tell the authorities. "If he refuses to listen to them," Jesus says, speaking of the witnesses, "tell it to the church" (Matt. 18:17). If your neighbor won't listen to you after you've spoken to him privately and then come with witnesses, there is no alternative but to make it public—not by noising the wrong all over the neighborhood, but by speaking to the authorities. If it is someone in your congregation, take it to the pastor or the council. If it is someone in your class, talk to your teacher. If it is something for the police, speak with them. One of these authorities can then take the proper steps to make sure the problem is laid to rest.

You see what great care God takes to protect our names. He not only forbids betraying, slandering, and lying about one another but he commands us to speak the truth in love, loving our neighbors enough to keep quiet about their faults unless we speak to them directly.

God is so concerned about our names because of the freedom in a good name: the freedom to live and serve well, confident of people's acceptance and respect. He'll protect your name and your neighbors' names to the end, keeping his earth ready for the day when the old Adam—with all of his name dropping and name destroying—dies forever.

Chapter 9

Counterfeit Hope

THE NINTH COMMANDMENT

You shall not covet your neighbor's house.

What does this mean for us?
We are to fear and love God so that we do not desire
to get our neighbor's possessions by scheming,
or by pretending to have a right to them,
but always help him keep what is his.

THE TENTH COMMANDMENT

**You shall not covet your neighbor's wife,
or his manservant, or his maidservant,
or his cattle, or anything that is
your neighbor's.**

What does this mean for us?
We are to fear and love God so that we do not tempt
or coax away from our neighbor his wife or his
workers, but encourage them to remain loyal.

Have you ever wished that you were someone else? Have you lain awake at night thinking about what it might be like if you were a little taller or shorter, a little stronger or faster, a little prettier or not quite so heavy—like someone else you know? Have you ever daydreamed about winning some special kind of honor? Or have you ever gone to sleep dreaming about what a difference it would make to have something special— a driver's license and a car, maybe a new stereo, some special clothes, a camera, a shotgun, shortwave radio, or something else?

Dreams and daydreams are full of hope—that's something else we can't live without. Hope is having something to look forward to, something to wait for tomorrow, the day after, and in the days to come. It is as necessary to us as life and breath— as our homes, property, and names.

Having made his decision about us in Christ, God gives us all kinds of hope. He gives us hope for the new day coming, the final day when he will have the last word and bring in his kingdom. And in the meantime, he gives us hope in his promise that he will care for us each day, giving us everything we could possibly need to live and serve him and our neighbors.

The old Adam knows how important hope is, too. But since he doesn't have any himself, he offers a counterfeit in its place. It's centered not on God's promise, but on yourself. The old Adam's counterfeit is coveting—setting your heart on someone or something that belongs to another person.

This false hope is often hidden in your daydreams and wishes. That may seem strange. There doesn't seem to be anything wrong with wishing or dreaming. It can inspire you to work hard, to go places and accomplish things. Dreaming is good in a lot of ways.

You know by now, though, that the old Adam is the master of counterfeiting and disguise. He hides himself in what looks good to have his way. That's why God has given two commandments to go after something as innocent looking as wishing.

First of all, as long as the old Adam is filling you and your neighbor with wishes for things you think you need to make your life complete, neither one of you is safe. Secondly, the old Adam uses his counterfeit hopes to make a slave of you and finally to burn you out. Then there is no hope.

Fencing the wish

If you've watched the commercials on television instead of running to the refrigerator—or somewhere else—during the program breaks, you've already seen some good examples of how dangerous wishes can be.

Take car commercials, for example. No matter how fancy or expensive the cars may be, they can only do one thing: haul you from one place to another. Some are large, some small; some get better mileage; some worse; some are more reliable than others. But there isn't one of them that can make you any sexier, any more intelligent, any more beautiful or handsome than you already are.

You wouldn't know that from the commercials, though. Each year the car companies spend hundreds of thousands of dollars and more to convince you and your parents that buying their model will change your life—that it will make you more distinguished, elegant, beautiful, daring, or desirable.

That is how coveting works. The advertising is legal but underhanded, designed to make you think that you have to have a certain car to be the person you want to be. The car companies covet your money, and use the tricks of advertising to make you covet one of their cars.

Another example of coveting happens in friendships. There is no law that says friendships have to last forever. There is nothing illegal about a third person wanting to become a friend of one of your friends, either. But if that third person tries to come between you and your friend, using tricks and schemes to do it, there is something wrong no matter how legal it is. Though the third person may not break any of the commandments, the tricks the person uses can separate you from a close friend and leave you alone.

The purpose of these commandments, then, is to close up these kinds of legal loopholes. We don't consider wives property, as people once did. Very few people have manservants and maidservants, and most people don't have cattle, either. But there are all kinds of tricks and schemes the old Adam can and does use to sneak through the other commandments, keeping all the appearances legal while working to deprive you of what is rightfully yours.

That's why coveting is so dangerous. When you want what belongs to your neighbors, they aren't safe. When they want what belongs to you, you aren't safe either. Even if the desires don't turn to outright adultery, theft or tricks, wanting something or someone who belongs to another person is the first step toward trying to take it away. When you want what belongs to others and others want what belongs to you, you can't be together without envy and suspicion.

So, by forbidding coveting, God works to maintain order in our communities. When covetousness is broken, we can wait and work with our neighbors, helping one another to keep what we have, looking forward together to the day when God will bring in the new day. That is real hope—not a counterfeit that makes us envious and suspicious of our neighbors.

The bad penny comes back

Like counterfeit money, the old Adam's wishes don't just cause trouble for neighbors—they come back to haunt you. Only it's worse than haunting—your wishes can make a slave of you and give you a worse enemy than you've dreamed of.

Take a car, for instance. Suppose the ads succeed in convincing you that if only you can get your hands on one special car, your whole life will change—that the car will make other people more interested in you; that you'll be sexier, happier, a real man or a real woman if you buy and drive it.

How would you go about getting such a car? Obviously, you couldn't steal it—if you did, you couldn't drive it around town. And the car companies are too smart and too big to be tricked. Somehow, you would have to find the money to buy it.

Then what would happen? Well, pretty soon your whole life would be devoted to getting enough money for that car. You'd make sacrifices, working after school, on Saturdays, and perhaps on Sundays, saving every penny you could lay your hands on. There would be little time for friendships, school, or having fun.

If you finally got the car, it might succeed in making you the envy of your school, town, or neighborhood at first. But pretty soon you'd wonder if all those people were interested in you or your car. More than likely you'd have to show that no other car nearby was better than yours. And you'd probably worry that someone might put sugar in your tank or do some other kind of damage out of envy.

Besides that, you'd have as much work on your hands as ever: making money to buy fuel, washing, waxing, shining and maintaining the car. Again there wouldn't be time for school work; not even enough time to drive the car around; no friends but those who really like the car.

It might sound like an attractive kind of slavery—having a car like that could be a lot of fun. But it would be a slavery just the same, wouldn't it? Everything would have to be organized and sacrificed for the wish—that beautiful slave maker. That's probably why so many people who get cars like that get tired of them after awhile. The wish, which started out as an innocent daydream, has made them slaves.

Cars aren't the only culprits. There are as many slave makers as there are things to covet. Athletes who covet prizes and the recognition they can bring can become blue ribbon slaves. The same thing happens to people who covet being beautiful. They spend all kinds of time grooming and primping to look just right, they buy only the latest fashions in clothes and don't feel comfortable in anything else, they always have to worry about how they look and what others think of them. They might be beautiful, but they are as much slaves as the ones who wear chains.

69

Every one of the old Adam's counterfeit hopes promises some kind of joy, some special recognition or honor, some special reward. And every one of them eventually falls short. The fancy car is soon outdated or it rusts and wears out. Athletes lose games and are soon forgotten. The beautiful people soon find out that beauty isn't everything or that they aren't as beautiful as they thought.

When these hopes burn out, the old Adam has to run out and find other counterfeits to take their places. They burn out, too. Finally it looks as though every hope is counterfeit and we're burned out entirely, hopeless, full of despair, certain that nothing is any fun anymore.

That's the second reason God forbids coveting—to protect us from ourselves. We are our own worst enemies, suckers for just about every counterfeit hope the old Adam drags in front of us.

Protecting us from ourselves

So God, as a gracious and loving father, works to protect us from ourselves by forbidding these kinds of wishes before they can get off the ground. "You shall not covet," he says. "Don't set your hearts on what belongs to your neighbors—not on the people who belong to them, not on the things that belong to them, not on the recognition, honor, or praise they can give you."

But God doesn't stop after he's said no. He says NO to the old Adam's false hopes because he is saying a much bigger YES to the new you, giving you a hope that won't fail. He has decided to be your God, to give you and all of us a hope that is real, not counterfeit. It is the hope of his promise that there is a new day coming when he will dwell with us, wiping out death, every tear, all mourning, sorrow, and pain.

God gives wishes, dreams, and hopes in the meantime, too: everything we could wish for, dream of, or hope for to help our neighbors. In fact, that's the only limit he sets on our wishing: that it not be at our neighbor's expense or our own. He's going to be our God, after all, right up to the day when he raises us from the dead and forever after. With that promise, he makes everything we need a gift.

Chapter 10

A Jealous God

**What does God say of all these commandments?
He says:**

"I, the Lord your God, am a jealous God,
visiting the iniquity of the fathers upon the
children to the third and fourth generation
of those who hate me, but showing steadfast
love to thousands of those who love me
and keep my commandments."

What does this mean for us?

God warns that he will punish all who break these
commandments. Therefore we are to fear his wrath
and not disobey him. But he promises grace and every
blessing to all who keep these commandments.
Therefore we are to love and trust him,
and gladly do what he commands.

Jealousy seems like a word better fit for soap operas and
mushy love stories than the almighty God. God jealous? Can
you imagine him worried sick that someone might not love him?
Or playing "she loves me—she loves me not" by picking a daisy-
shaped star apart piece by piece? The God of the promise jealous?

But God says it himself: "I, the Lord your God, am a jealous God." It's not a mistaken translation, either. In fact, if you could read Hebrew you'd find a word even stronger than jealous. The original word suggests burning like an unquenchable fire. Can you imagine that? God hot for you? Burning like a white hot flame with desire for you?

There's a more polite word for it, even if it seems tame by comparison. It is love. Lovers are the ones who get jealous. That's what stands behind God's jealousy, too. He loves you. He has made his decision about you, about you and his whole creation: he is going to be your God and bring in his new day.

The trouble is that God has all sorts of rivals competing for you—rivals who want to come between him and you. Not one of them is anywhere near as great or strong as he is, of course, but that's why God is jealous. He won't tolerate anyone or anything else claiming your fear, love, and trust.

That's why he has attached a terrible threat and an even greater promise to the Ten Commandments. He makes both the threat and the promise for the same reason—because he loves you, he is determined to make you his own.

The threat and the promise

The threat comes first: "I, the Lord your God, am a jealous God, visiting the iniquity of the fathers upon the children to the third and fourth generation of those who hate me. . . ." That's awfully strong medicine. In fact, it sounds unfair—that children should suffer not only for the sins of their fathers but of their grandparents, great-grandparents, and great-great-grandparents.

You know by now, though, that the old Adam is no joke. If he isn't anywhere near as strong as God, he is still powerful enough to hold us in a grip we can't break.

The old Adam in us makes us concerned first, foremost, and always about ourselves. He is the one who frightens and worries us, convincing us that if we don't look out for ourselves, no one else will. In each of the commandments now, you've seen how he struggles, squirms, and fights in us to put himself between God and us and between our neighbors and ourselves. If he ever got completely out of hand, doing everything he wished in us and others, it would split the earth into billions of pieces.

To prevent that, and to keep the earth ready for his promise, God has given us the commandments. He ties such an awful threat to them for the same reason. Because the old Adam is so selfish, the only way he'll listen is if he knows something terrible is going to happen to him if he keeps it up. So God threatens. It's as if he says, "Look, if you're going to insist on your selfish ways, you're going to live with the consequences."

God is far too kind to ever let us live with all of the consequences of the old Adam's work in us. But he won't be mocked, either. Nor will he spoil us, coming like an overly indulgent father or mother to bail us out of whatever scrapes we get ourselves into. If you treat your parents with contempt and disobey them, God isn't going to prevent them from punishing you. In fact, he encourages them to do so. If you kill someone, God isn't going to come to the police station to plead for your release. You live with the consequences of your own actions.

The consequences can keep going, too. For instance, when fathers and mothers sin against their children by not giving them the proper love and care, the children are hurt by it. When they become parents themselves, it is hard for them to learn how to give the kind of love and care to their children they didn't get from their own parents. Thus the grandchildren can be hurt by what their grandparents did to their parents.

God isn't keeping books, looking to get even with you for something your great-great-grandpa or grandma did. He gra-

ciously forgives, never letting us live with all the consequences of wrong. But he lets us live with enough of them to let us know that he's not making empty threats. As long as the old Adam in you insists on selfishness, you'll have to live with its results. It is as if God says, "If you won't listen to these commandments for my sake, listen to them for your own. If you don't, you'll have to live with it."

God uses the promise he attaches to the commandments in the same way. But the promise is much bigger than the threat: "I, the Lord your God, am a jealous God . . . showing steadfast love to thousands of those who love me and keep my commandments." That's quite a difference, isn't it? Iniquity to three or four generations—steadfast love to thousands?

But it almost sounds as if God is trying to make a deal, promising to "show steadfast love" *if* you love him and keep his commandments. That's not like him, is it?

God knows what he's doing. He knows the old Adam can never resist a bargain. So he takes hold of the selfishness in us and says, "Look, if you won't hear the commandments for my sake, listen to them for your own good—I'm going to show mercy to thousands of generations of those who love me. If you want to get in on it, you'd better give it a try."

Both the threat and the promise have the same purpose, then.

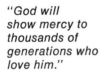

"God will show mercy to thousands of generations who love him."

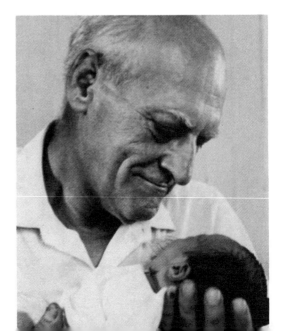

God puts them together with the commandments as parents put spankings and rewards together with their commands. They are temporary measures to hold the old Adam in line while the new you comes forth.

While their children are young and don't know any better, good parents give commands—telling the children what they should and shouldn't do. The parents back up their commands with spankings and rewards when they need to, making sure that their children don't hurt themselves and others.

All the while, though, the parents are looking forward to the day when commands, spankings, and rewards won't be necessary anymore. Then the children will be mature enough to know what is good and right themselves.

That's what God is looking forward to for us. For the time being, while the old Adam is at work, God gives commandments, using threats and promises to back them up. He uses them to protect us from ourselves and our neighbors, keeping his creation ready for his promise.

One day God is going to put the old Adam to death permanently, and make the whole world new. Then Christ will reign and there will be no more old Adam, no more death, no more commands, threats, or bargains. Then he will raise us up as his new people to "live with him in righteousness and purity forever."

The promise and the purpose

In the meantime, the Ten Commandments are precious gifts for us. Through them, we see how God cares for us day by day, showing his promise and purpose for us.

The most important commandment by far is the First. It is "the clasp that holds the wreath together," as Luther called it. In it, God gives us his word that he will be our God, give us everything good, and care for us at all times. "I am the Lord your God," he says. "You shall have no other gods before me."

All the rest of the commandments follow from this one. Because God promises to be our God, he gives us his name and speaks to us through his word. Because he is our God, God protects our lives in every way, seeing to it that not only life itself but everything we need to live—including faithful companions, property, good names and sound hopes—is kept for us.

At the same time, the First Commandment opens up all the others to show us God's purposes for us. Because God promises to be our God, he expects us to fear, love, and trust him above all things. And because he is our God, God also expects us to care for our neighbors, protecting and helping them.

Jesus summed up these purposes and all the commandments in two: "You shall love the Lord your God with all your heart, and with all your soul, and with all your mind," he said. And "You shall love your neighbor as yourself. On these two commandments depend all the law and the prophets" (Matt. 22:37-40). That's why we're made—those are our purposes for living.

When the old Adam hears such big commandments and sees such huge purposes, he ignores the promise and starts complaining about the load. "How can God expect so much?" he asks with a scowl. "I could never do all that."

"That's right," God says, "you can't." There isn't a man, woman, or child alive who can keep these commandments as they are meant to be kept, perfectly and completely.

God is at work

But God isn't waiting for us to keep them under our own steam, as if the commandments were blanks on a test we had to fill in before God would care for us. He's already decided what he's going to do with us, and he's been at work since our Baptisms to do it. He's putting the old Adam in each of us to death and raising us up as new people.

That's what we're going to be—new people. God is making the new you in you, the you who will be a believer, the you who fears, loves and trusts him. He is making the new you in you who will be a lover, one who loves each neighbor. He is making the new you in you who will be what Adam and Eve were made to be, one who cares for the earth.

But now there are some questions left. How do we know what God's decision is for us? And how is he going to make us what we will be? It's these questions that we'll consider as we discuss the Apostles' Creed. It, too, is packed full and running over with God's promises. It is a joyous declaration of how God cares for us as our Father, of all that he does for us in Christ, and of how he sends his Spirit to make and keep the new you.

Chapter 11

I Believe

If God were the kind of God most people seem to think he is, worried always and only about whether we're doing what we should do, he would have stopped after giving us the Ten Commandments. They give us plenty to do—more than we could ever accomplish in a lifetime of hard trying. They also give us plenty of protection—if not all the protection we might want, at least enough so that most people can expect to live a good many years.

If that was all God was interested in, he could have gone home from Mt. Sinai, pulled up an easy chair, and spent the rest of the time watching us struggle and squirm trying to do what he told us to do.

But God isn't that kind of God. You already know that—he himself made it clear right away, in the First Commandment. Instead of sitting around waiting for you to do something to show that you are good enough for him, he came right out and said, "I am the Lord your God. You shall have no other gods."

He has said it before—he'll say it again. "I've decided about you," he says. "I'm going to be your God, look after and protect you, and give you every good thing. I'm going to make you and the whole creation new."

What kind of God is he, then? What is he like? What does he do and what can we expect from him? The Apostles' Creed contains the answers to these questions. It tells us how God has made himself known to us, letting us know who he is and what he does. Through the Creed, in fact, we learn "to know God perfectly," as Luther put it.

God makes himself known

But how does this happen? How do we get to know God? Some suppose that we get to know God as we get to know any other person. We "find" him and then use our abilities to observe and reason, to figure him out.

If we start out this way, trying on our own to get a picture of who God is and what he's like, we run into a solid wall right away. "No one has ever seen God," as John says in his Gospel (1:18). Not even Moses, who spoke with God on Mt. Sinai, could see his face (Exod. 33:17-23).

If we can't see him, how can we get to know God? We can't sit down with him and ask questions as we could if he were another person. We can't go places or do things with him either, as you might do with someone you wanted to get acquainted with at school.

There might be a door in the wall, though. If we can't see God, maybe we can "find" him by looking at the world around us, observing what happens, and reasoning back from there.

Think of the order and balance in nature, for instance. Spring, summer, autumn, and winter come year after year like clockwork; birds, flowers, animals, plants, and people live in an intricate web of life; in a whole universe full of stars, moons, suns, and planets, everything works together. Surely there must be a God behind it all.

But what kind of God? That's really the question. If we ask nature for an answer, we may get one, but it may be far different from what we expect.

Nature can be beautiful—that's for sure. But there are some other things for sure, too. "Mother Nature" can be cruel and ruthless, with tornadoes, cyclones, blizzards, and earthquakes that kill and maim. And that intricate web of life is also a web of death—animals killing and being killed in the fight to survive.

What kind of God do we "find" if we try to peek at him through nature? A God who can be as warm as the summer sunshine and as beautiful as the first flower in the spring, but also as cold as winter ice and as relentless as the death of the leaves in the autumn. No wonder people who try to "find" God in this way give him such cold and lifeless names: Supreme Being, Unmoved Mover, First Cause.

We can't see God. Though we might catch a few glimpses of him in nature or in what happens to us, we can't get a picture of who he is or what he really does in this way. Trying to know him on our own, by our observations and reasoning, we run smack into a wall we can't break through.

It is God's own wall we run into—a wall of mirrors. You remember how the old Adam operates. He is the old you in you who always wants to go it alone, to have you figure out things for yourself, without help from God or your neighbors. He wants to find God so that he can either get rid of him or use him in some way.

That's why God has put up this wall of mirrors. When the old Adam tries to get God's measure, to pry into his secrets, to

get a jump on him, God shines the mirrors in his face so that the only picture the old Adam gets is of himself.

What about it, then? Are we stymied before we start? How are we going to get to know God at all, much less perfectly, if he's hidden behind a wall of mirrors?

We cannot get to know God *on our own*, by our own reason or strength, effort or understanding. But if God *makes himself known*, helping us to know him, then we can know him better than we know our own selves.

God does just that. He doesn't wait for us to find him. He doesn't play hard to get, like a bashful stranger, hoping we'll try to get acquainted with him. Rather, he makes himself known, telling us who he is, what he does, and what we can expect from him.

If you remember the Second and Third Commandments, you already have a pretty good idea of how God does this. He makes himself known through his word, in events, as he did with Abraham, Isaac, Jacob, and the prophets. But above all, God makes himself known in Christ.

In Christ, God didn't stand far off in the distance, shouting at us about all we're supposed to do. He became one of us, like us,

our own flesh and blood. In him, God didn't sit in a heavenly hammock arranging events and pulling nature's strings like some coldly competent computer. Rather, he took upon himself the most wretched and terrifying things we know, suffering, dying, going all the way to the grave for us. In Christ, God shattered death's chains and broke the grave wide open, raising him from the dead.

Not just talk

That's how God makes himself known to us. He didn't just talk about himself. He did what he does, he "did" himself, for us. He himself came to be with us to make us know what kind of God he is, what he does, and what we can expect him to do.

What kind of God is he then? In Christ, we learn that God is the one who gives eyes to the blind, ears to the deaf, voices to the mute, legs to the lame, health to the sick, life to the dead. He is the one who loves his enemies—the unrighteous and the impious and the super righteous and the super pious alike. He is the one who forgives and raises the dead; the one who by word and deed makes all things new. He is God.

Once we begin to know what God is like in Christ, we can begin to see his hand more clearly in the creation, too. Apart from Christ, the creation—this earth and everything with it—is a big mystery. It is a huge system of rules and laws, of accidents and coincidences, that seems to run by luck.

Christ doesn't wipe away the mystery, telling us why things happen the way they do, why there is suffering, death, anguish, and pain. But he does tell us who it is that made our world and daily cares for it—his Father, and ours. That makes all the difference.

God doesn't just tell us about creation, giving us another science lesson. He *does* creation. He made the earth and he cares for it. He clothes the lilies of the field, feeds the birds of the air, and gives you what you need, guarding and protecting you from day to day. He is himself when he is creating something out of nothing, when he is making all things new.

When we see how God makes himself known to us in Christ, we learn something else about him, too: that he really wants us to know him. He wasn't content to be the unknown God hidden in some far-off heaven. He wasn't content to make himself known to a few people living in a tiny corner of the world 2000 years ago, either. He wants to make himself known to you, to each of us, to all of us, right now.

So he sends his Spirit, the Holy Spirit, to make himself known through his word. He "does" himself again, telling the story of Jesus to us, telling us who he is and what he is going to make of us.

What is God like? He is the God who promises and keeps his word. He is like no other person, no thing, no power you have ever known. Instead of waiting for you to find him, waiting for you to prove yourself worthy of him, he makes himself known to you.

He repeats himself, doing himself three times to tell you who he is, what he does, and what you can expect from him. He is God the Father almighty, the Maker of heaven and earth. He is Jesus Christ, his only Son, our Lord. He is the Holy Spirit. He is the triune God, one in three, three in one.

"In Christ, God shattered death's chains."

God makes himself known so that each of us can say, "I believe." That's what the Apostles' Creed is for, too. It is a very ancient creed—most of it was put together by 340 A.D. and probably even earlier. It has been used ever since, with only a few additions in the early centuries of the church, for the same purpose: to tell people who are about to be baptized, or who have been baptized, *who* God is and *what* we receive and can expect from him.

The Creed was said at your Baptism, too, even though you probably couldn't understand it. It was said in confidence that God was making and will make you one of his own, enabling you yourself to say, "I believe."

That isn't always easy to say. In fact, it can be very difficult. The old Adam hangs around our necks trying to squeeze the faith out of us. He fills us with fear, despair, and pride in ourselves. He fills our world with suffering, pain, and death. Seeing that, watching what goes on in the world, it can be hard to believe the promise—sometimes almost impossible.

But that's what God is looking for, and that's what he's going to make of you: a believer. In the commandments, we saw how he keeps the old Adam on a leash to protect us and keep the world ready for the promise. Now, in the creed, we're going to see how the old Adam dies.

We're going to discover something else, too: how God makes himself known to raise up the new you in us, the new you who is a believer and can say, "I believe in God the Father almighty," in "Jesus Christ, his only Son our Lord," and in "the Holy Spirit."

Whoever can say that is being brought back to the point where Adam fell. In fact, as God enables you to say that, you are brought even further: to the point where you "know God perfectly," who he is, what he does, and what you can confidently expect from him. Think it will happen? Just wait.

Chapter 12

Not How but Who

THE FIRST ARTICLE
**I believe in God the Father almighty,
Maker of heaven and earth.**

What does this mean?
I believe that God has created me and all that
exists. He has given me and still preserves my body
and soul with all their powers. He provides me with
food and clothing, home and family, daily work,
and all I need from day to day. God also protects me
in time of danger and guards me from every evil.
All this he does out of fatherly and divine goodness
and mercy, though I do not deserve it. Therefore I
surely ought to thank and praise, serve and obey him.
This is most certainly true.

The big question tagging along behind the First Article is,
"How?" How did God make the heavens and the earth? And
how does he give us food, clothing, and everything else we need
from day to day?

There are good reasons for asking these questions. Knowing
how God makes life could open the door to all kinds of nature's
secrets. And knowing how God gives us everything we need

from day to day could make life a lot easier. As it is, there are plenty of things about life we don't know. And we do know it takes hard work and long hours to put food on the table, clothes on our backs, roofs over our heads.

But God seems intent on keeping these "how's" a secret, at least in the Creed and the Scriptures. Both of them are more than glad to say *who* made the earth and *who* gives us what we need—God the Father Almighty. But neither of them says *how*.

"In the beginning God made the heavens and the earth," Genesis says (1:1). How did he do it? With his word. "And God said, 'Let there be light'; and there was light" (Gen. 1:3). But how can words do that? No answer. There are no recipes provided; there is no stopping to explain the methods or means God used.

The same goes for the second question, How does God give us everything we need? The Creed is silent. The explanation in the Catechism only says that God does it. And again, the Bible doesn't say much more.

In fact, Jesus just turns the question around. "Look at the birds of the air: they neither sow nor reap nor gather into barns, and yet your heavenly Father feeds them. Are you not of more value than they?" And, "Consider the lilies of the field, how they grow; they neither toil nor spin; yet I tell you, even Solomon in all of his glory was not arrayed like one of these. . . . Will he not much more clothe you, O men of little faith?" (Matt. 6:26, 28-30).

It looks as if we've run into another wall, doesn't it? We may have good reasons for asking how, and there are many possible explanations. But there aren't any explanations in the Creed or the Bible. Maybe instead of asking them how, then, we should ask the question they insist on answering: Who? Who made the heavens and the earth? And who gives us everything we need from day to day?

The old Adam's answer

It was this question, "Who?" that started the rebellion in the Garden of Eden.

When God created Adam and Eve, one of the limits he placed on them was that they should not eat the fruit of one tree in the garden—"the tree of knowledge of good and evil" (Gen. 2:17). You know what happened next. Don't let the fact that Eve ate first put you off. When the tempter came with his wily suggestion, both Adam and Eve ate, and with a good appetite.

But the eating isn't the point of the story—rather it's the temptation. Note how many times the tempter said "you." "You will not die," he said. "For God knows that when you eat of it (the fruit), your eyes will be opened, and you will be like God, knowing good and evil" (Gen. 3:4-5).

This temptation might sound simple, but that's just what makes it so subtle and powerful. The snake caught Adam and

Eve with his answer to the question, "Who?" Who gives you everything you need from day to day? "*You* can," the snake said. "Just eat and you'll be able to get everything you need by yourself."

"Listen," the snake said, "if you eat of the tree of knowledge of good and evil, you'll be like God—you'll know what's good for you and what's bad for you and you'll be able to choose between them. You won't have to count on God for everything good—you'll be able to take care of yourself."

That's why the usual name for this story, "the fall," isn't the best one. The old Adam likes to call it a fall to make it sound as if he just slipped a few notches. He wants to make it look as if he's a religious athlete who just broke a few training rules or stole a few apples—that if only he'll feel bad about it and try harder he can pick himself up again and get back into God's good graces.

Rebellion

That's not it at all. It was, and is, a rebellion—an uprising. Adam and Eve listened to the voice of the tempter. They rose up against God and became his enemies. This uprising is repeated in us constantly, as over and over again, in countless different ways we say, "I'd rather do it myself." "I can do what I want to do."

That's how the old you in us operates. From the day we're born until the day we die, the old Adam convinces us that we know what is best for ourselves—that our will, what we want, what we like, and what we think should be made law. He tells us that we can and should take care of ourselves, providing what we need for ourselves and having our own way as much as possible.

What's wrong with that? If we don't take care of ourselves, who will? Who is going to give us what we need if we don't get it for ourselves? Isn't that just the question?

You know the Creed's answer, Christ's own answer: God the Father almighty, the God of the promise, the one who came right out and said, "I am the Lord your God. I will give you every good thing."

When God told Adam and Eve not to eat the fruit of the tree

of knowledge of good and evil, he wasn't just being arbitrary. He had a reason, his promise. He commanded them not to eat of it because he intended to take care of them himself.

And isn't that what God did? Adam and Eve didn't have any parents. They didn't make themselves, or somehow earn the right to life, either. God simply decided to make people and when he did, he gave life to Adam and Eve as his gift. And he surrounded them with other gifts—plants, animals, trees, flowers, a whole garden teeming with life. He cared for them, making sure they had plenty to eat, good company, and important jobs to do.

Hasn't God done the same for you? He didn't make you out of the dust of the ground, of course—you had parents. But you didn't earn the right to be born, either. Nor did you earn points or make promises so that some parents would finally volunteer to have you. Your life was given to you, as a gift.

You received some other gifts with it—you can think, read, sing, love, hope, dream; you have some special talents and abilities. Did you earn them? Not a chance—they were given to you. You are gifted.

And what about the food on your table? Your parents probably worked hard for it, earning money and spending time preparing it. But where was that food grown and raised? Who paid for the sunshine and the rain? Who provided the ground that crops could be raised in or cattle grazed on? There are a lot of gifts in your food.

And what about the clothes on your back? Whether cotton or rayon, wool or Dacron, didn't the cloth in those clothes start out

as a gift of the earth? You bet it did—in cotton fields, in an oil field, on a sheep's back. And what about your house or apartment? Didn't it start out as timber in the woods, as clay in the ground, as sand and lime and stone?

Your parents work hard, probably very hard, to earn money to buy what you need from day to day. Someday, you'll probably do the same. But even jobs are gifts. God has arranged his creation so that there's a gift in everything we are and have, in everything we do and receive.

Who gives life? Who gives you what you need from day to day? God does. God the Father almighty, the God of the promise.

There's another question that goes with Who: it is, "Why?" Why does God give us all these gifts? There can be only one answer to that question: "All this he does out of fatherly and divine goodness and mercy, though I do not deserve it."

If God ever started demanding payment in return, requiring us to give something in exchange for all of his gifts, there wouldn't be any more gifts. But he insists on giving. He gives us what we need from day to day because he wants to, because he has decided to, because he has promised to be our God.

But God has a purpose for us in his gifts, a purpose in mind for you: that you will thank and praise, serve and obey him. That's how the new you goes to work. In fact, that's what God made Adam and Eve for in the first place: to serve him in faith, to care for one another, to care for his garden.

We are made for faith—to rely on God for everything good while we go about our jobs. We're created to be believers, to count on God to keep his word, to care for all he has made—not in trade but for the joy of it, because he is God and we are his.

The old Adam is the one who keeps asking how. Like Adam and Eve, he wants to break into God's secrets so that he can help us to help ourselves. So he peppers the first article with "how's." How did God make the heavens and the earth? And how is he going to give you what you need each day when the world is full of hunger, despair, poverty, defeat, and depression?

But you know something that's far more important. You know who made the heavens and the earth, who gives you every gift. It is the God who said, "I am the Lord your God," the God who became your God at your Baptism.

90

Chapter 13

Mystery Man

THE SECOND ARTICLE

**And in Jesus Christ his only Son, our Lord;
who was conceived by the Holy Ghost,
born of the Virgin Mary; suffered under
Pontius Pilate, was crucified, dead and
buried; he descended into hell; the third day
he rose again from the dead; he ascended into
heaven, and sitteth on the right hand of God
the Father almighty; from thence he shall
come to judge the quick and the dead.**

What does this mean?

I believe that Jesus Christ—true God,
son of the Father from eternity, and true man,
born of the Virgin Mary—is my Lord. At great cost
he has saved and redeemed me, a lost and condemned
person. He has freed me from sin, death, and the
power of the devil—not with silver or gold,
but with his holy and precious blood and his
innocent suffering and death. All this he has done
that I may be his own, live under him in his kingdom,
and serve him in everlasting righteousness,
innocence, and blessedness, just as he is risen
from the dead and lives and rules eternally.
This is most certainly true.

One of the best ways to ruin a good mystery story is to read the end before finishing the rest of it. Whether it is a book, comic book, or rerun on television, knowing how the story is going to turn out usually takes the fun out of it.

Some mysteries are different, though—especially good ones. They can tell you what the end of the story will be and still keep you on the edge of your chair wondering who really did it and how it happened.

The story of Jesus is like that. You already know the end of it—that Jesus was crucified, died, and was buried; that he was raised from the dead and will bring in the new creation. But knowing the end of the story doesn't take the mystery away. In fact, it may just make him and his story all the more mysterious.

Who really is Jesus? What kind of person is he? And what really happened in him?

In this chapter and the next, we're going to work with these questions and some different ways of answering them.

How do you get to know other people? By seeing them and hearing them, right? Or, if you can't do that, by listening to others who have seen or heard them.

That's one way we can learn something about Jesus. Though we can't see him or listen to him as we could if he were someone in the congregation or at school, we can listen to what the Gos-

pels tell us people saw and heard in him. If we do, we'll run straight into the mystery.

One of the first things the Gospels tell us about Jesus is that he was a person, a human being. Now, not everybody wants to start out by saying this, or even to say it at all. Some say that Jesus just looked like a man or pretended he was one. Others say that he was so great that he couldn't have been just a human being.

But that's how the Gospels speak of him, and that's how the people he walked and talked with saw him. They saw a real man. "Where did this man get this wisdom and these mighty works?" the people of Nazareth asked. "Is not this the carpenter's son? Is not his mother called Mary? And are not his brothers James and Joseph and Simon and Judas? And are not all his sisters with us? Where then did this man get all this?" (Matthew 13:54-56).

He was a man. That's part of what made him such a mystery.

The Creed insists on it, too: that no matter what else can and should be said about Jesus, he was a real live human being. He was "born of the Virgin Mary," the Creed says. The most important word is "born"—born as you were born, as all human beings are born. So, as the explanation in the Catechism says, he was "true man," a real person.

But what kind of person? One of the next things the Gospels tells us about him is that he was a preacher. Does that sound too common and ordinary? It shouldn't, because that's what Jesus did.

What did Jesus preach? Mark summed it up this way: "The time is fulfilled," Jesus said, "and the kingdom of God is at hand; repent, and believe in the gospel" (Mark 1:15). He proclaimed and promised it again and again: that God himself is coming to make the new you and the new creation.

A preacher of good news

"The Spirit of the Lord is upon me," Jesus said, reading from the book of Isaiah to the people in Nazareth, "because he has anointed me to preach good news to the poor. He has sent me to proclaim release to the captives and recovering of sight to the blind, to set at liberty those who are oppressed, to proclaim the acceptable year of the Lord" (Luke 4:18-21).

That's just exactly what Jesus did. He proclaimed good news to the poor, going from town to town and table to table, telling all kinds of people about God's decision to make them and the creation new. He proclaimed release to the old Adam's captives —religious people who fancied themselves in some kind of special favor with God; irreligious people who were despised and condemned. He accepted and called prostitutes and other sinners to a changed life. He sat and ate with tax collectors like Zacchaeus who had made a fortune cheating, and radicals like Simon the Zealot, one of his disciples, who wanted to start a revolution to drive out all the Romans.

Wherever Jesus went, he made people new. He gave sight to the blind—people like old Bartimaeus who sat begging by the roadside as Jesus went to Jerusalem. He set at liberty people who were oppressed—like the paralyzed man who was lowered to him through the roof of a house, or like the men whose bodies were rotten with the disease of leprosy and who couldn't enjoy the company of others because of their illness. He healed the sick and raised the dead, driving out demons and making people new by just saying the word.

That's what made Jesus such a mystery, not only to the people of Nazareth but to others wherever he went. That's what can make him so mysterious to us, too. He was a man—nobody who saw him had any doubt about that. He was a preacher— everybody who heard him knew that, too.

But how could he make everything and everybody who listened new by just saying the word? Who was he, that he could stride through Galilee preaching God's decision about his people and his creation?

Not even his family and disciples—the people who knew him best—could figure him out completely. His family once tried to seize him and take him home (Mark 3:21). And his disciples misunderstood him again and again (Mark 8:14-21, for instance).

Other preachers and teachers in Israel, as well as the Romans, had an answer, though. To them he was more than a mystery— he was a threat. The religious leaders took Jesus for a blasphemer, a false preacher who takes God's name in vain.

The Romans apparently took him for another radical freedom

fighter. They were the only ones in Israel who could condemn a man to death. And that's what they did. He suffered under the authority of Pontius Pilate, the Roman governor. He was crucified, dead, and buried—put to death the way runaway slaves, criminals, and rebels were killed.

Who does he think he is?

There's another way that we can try to get to the bottom of the mystery. We can try to figure out from the Gospels who Jesus thinks he is. That will work with some people. You can come straight out and ask, "Who are you?" and get an answer. If we do that with Jesus, though, the mystery only deepens.

The mystery is that in only one verse in the first three Gospels does Jesus come right out and say that he is the Christ. Other people often say that he is. For instance, when Jesus asked his disciples, "Who do you say I am?" Peter replied, "You are the Christ" (Mark 8:29). And after he was crucified, the captain of the Roman soldiers who put him to death said, "Truly this man was the Son of God" (Mark 15:39).

But Jesus said it only once, and then in a puzzling way. When he was on trial the high priest asked him, "'Are you the Christ, the Son of the Blessed?' And Jesus said, 'I am; and you will see the Son of man seated at the right hand of power, and coming with the clouds of heaven'" (Mark 14:61).

Don't you think that's kind of strange? It's almost as if Jesus shrugged his shoulders and said, "Sure I am, but just wait until you see the Son of man coming. That will really be something." It sounds as though Jesus was trying to make it mysterious.

Sometimes people don't talk about themselves for good reason —it sounds like bragging. Jesus said as much himself: "If I bear witness to myself, my testimony is not true" (John 5:31). Maybe that's why he didn't come right out and say who he was. Maybe instead of talking about himself, he let us know who he is in another way: by what he did.

Just run through the Gospels, watching what he does. He goes all over Galilee and finally to Jerusalem preaching God's decision and promise to make the new creation. He heals the sick, drives out demons, forgives sins, and raises the dead, making people new wherever he finds them. And when he gets to Jerusalem, he doesn't fight or organize the disciples to protect him. He surrenders and lets the people who want to do away with him carry him to his death.

The clue

That's the clue: to watch what Jesus does and what happens to him. When you do, you'll see an entirely different kind of person—the *new* Adam. Where the old Adam is always trying to take care of himself, to get and grab as much as he can, Jesus lets go of himself, pouring himself out for us. He reverses the old Adam's direction, giving himself completely instead of trying to hold on to himself.

We'll follow up this clue in the next chapter. In the meantime, while we've run into a mystery, we've gained some important information.

First of all, Jesus was a man, a real live human being: in fact, as the *new* Adam, the only truly human being. Second, he was a preacher—a man who proclaimed God's promise and put the promise into action, making all kinds of people new. And third, he didn't say very much about who he is, but let his action do the talking for him.

Chapter 14

Friend of Sinners

Who is Jesus? So far, we have a mystery and a clue. He was a person—a man. And he was a preacher.

But he was an amazing one. He not only said that God had decided to make his creation new—he went to work all over Galilee and finally in Jerusalem doing just that, making people new. Who in the world was he that he could say and do such amazing things? That's the question, the mystery of Jesus.

We have one big clue to go on. When it comes to the question of who he is, Jesus lets his action do the talking. The clue, then, is to keep eyes open and ears to the ground to catch the action in his story—what Jesus does and what happens to him.

When we do that, we run into the biggest events in Jesus' story—the cross and the resurrection. There's a lot of mystery in them, too, but they throw light on the whole story of Jesus. They tell us who he is and what happened in him, how the old Adam dies and the new age begins.

The lights of Easter

Jesus was dead. He hung on the cross until he died. When the soldiers took him down to haul his body away, they made sure there was no mistake about it—spearing him in the side to drain the lifeblood out of him. His body was taken and buried in another man's tomb—sealed in a cave behind a stone.

The disciples and those who had followed Jesus thought it was the end of the mystery. They thought he was just one more good man who had said and done some amazing things, but who died like everyone else.

Jesus didn't treat his dying as just one more chapter in a mystery, either, or as something unpleasant that he had to do for a little while. At Gethsemane the night before, Mark says that Jesus was "greatly distressed and troubled" (14:33), praying three times that it wouldn't be necessary to suffer and die in such a way. And when he did die, Jesus cried out in pain and agony, "My God, my God, why hast thou forsaken me?" (Mark 15:34). He wasn't pretending, or just giving up his life for a weekend. He died.

Mary Magdalene, Mary the mother of James, and Salome thought the mystery was over, too, when they went to the grave on Easter morning. They didn't go to see if Jesus really would be raised. They went to wash his body with oils and spices so that it wouldn't smell of death.

When they got there, the women got the surprise of their lives —the biggest surprise in all of history. The tomb was empty! Jesus had been raised from the dead. He *is* risen! Later on, others saw and spoke with him. He appeared to Peter and the disciples, to 500 of those who had followed him, to James and the apostles, and finally to Paul (1 Cor. 15:3-8).

Now there is a lot of mystery in the resurrection, too. All kinds of fascinating questions can be asked about it. But in all of the mystery, two things are most important: that Jesus was crucified and that God raised him from the dead.

Together, these events are like the sun. Though we can't look at them directly, with naked eyes, we can see the light they shed. Good Friday and Easter light up the mystery, telling us who Jesus is and why he died. And they light up the future, the dawning of the new age.

When the disciples saw and heard Jesus risen from the dead, they set out to preach him to all who would listen. They proclaimed him in a short and simple creed: "Jesus is Lord."

That's the light the resurrection sheds on the mystery of who Jesus is: he is Lord, God himself in the flesh of a person like us, God being himself, doing what he does, for us. Jesus is "true God, son of the Father from eternity," as the explanation in the Catechism says.

Why all the mystery, then? Why didn't Jesus come right out at the beginning and say himself that he is God?

"If I bear witness to myself, my testimony is not true," Jesus said (John 5:31). But there's more to it, too. Do you love someone who is always lording it over you, telling you what you have to do whether you like it or not? Someone who is always rippling

99

muscles to prove that he can pound you to pulp if or when he wants to?

Can you see it now? God is making believers, people who will love him wholeheartedly, for himself, with nothing held back.

How's God going to make that kind of love? Not with force—love can't be forced. Not by scaring you—you don't love people you're afraid of. No, he'll get it by setting aside all of his power, glory, honor, and might to become a person, just like you, as he has done in Christ! By becoming a person who laughs and who struggles, as you do. By becoming poor, weak, humble and sorrowful, as we often are. By sitting down to the table and taking food with the wretched and despised—prostitutes, traitors, radicals, cowards, pretenders, puppy lovers, the unrighteous and the ungodly of all kinds. That's just what Jesus did.

The cross was no mistake

But why did he have to die, then? In the light of Easter, we can see that, too. In Christ, God wasn't willing to go halfway for us. He went all the way, giving himself completely, withholding nothing, to break the old Adam's grip and make us his own.

The cross wasn't a mistake or an accident. It happened on purpose, the way Christ wanted it to.

When a person is found in the company of thieves, what happens to him? He is picked up and accused of the same crimes as the thieves, isn't he? He becomes what the law sometimes calls an "accessory after the fact," a befriender of criminals. And though he may be completely innocent, he may very well get the thieves' punishment. That's the way the law works.

If you were picked up like that, more than likely you'd yell and protest, telling everybody who would listen how unfair it is to be accused of something you didn't do. But what if you really loved the people you were with? That would make quite a difference, wouldn't it?

That was Jesus' "crime"—his love. He wasn't a bystander who just happened to get caught with some bad company. He *wanted* to be in bad company. He wanted to be the friend of sinners—not only of thieves, prostitutes, tax collectors, revolutionaries, and other criminals, but of all kinds of sinners.

And when he was condemned to die for it, Jesus didn't go

kicking and screaming to the cross, crying out about the unfairness of it. Though it was a dreadful suffering and a horrible death, he *wanted* it that way—to take upon himself the sins, punishment and death of his friends, his people—each of us. He bore our sins in his body. He died in our place, for us.

Was he trying to buy God off, then? Trying to satisfy God's anger in some way? You know better—God is no trader, no swapper who can be bought for a price. He isn't for sale no matter how high the price might be.

Jesus gave himself like a loving mother would give herself if she threw herself in front of a speeding car to protect her child

*"How does God make
you a believer?
By becoming a
person like you."*

playing in the street. A mother who did such a thing wouldn't be making a sacrifice *to* someone—she would be making a sacrifice *for* someone, her child.

Jesus' death isn't a sacrifice *to* God—it is God's sacrifice *for* us. Jesus laid down his life for us, giving everything, withholding nothing, dying condemned and abandoned, to set us free. That is love—love that "does not insist on its own way," that "does not rejoice at wrong but rejoices in the right," love that "bears all things" for us (1 Cor. 13:5-7).

The new you and the new age

Someday you will die, as Jesus did—not on a cross, most likely, but somewhere, somehow. Sometimes it can seem far away, sometimes close at hand and frightening. But it's the fundamental law of life: every living thing, no matter what or who it is, must die.

In Christ's word, the word of his death and resurrection, you hear a new word that breaks this law of death. It is a word spoken by the same God who created the heavens and the earth; the same God who became a person, who suffered and died and was raised from the dead in Christ.

This new word is a promise: though you die, you will live. It is the word of the cross and Easter: as Christ died for you, he lives for you to make you and his creation new. That's the light that shines into the future, lighting it up for you, showing you what is to come.

Christ's death and resurrection are the old Adam's death. It is like a great battle. Christ came armed with grace and truth and every blessing. The old Adam came armed with sin and death and every curse, determined to get rid of God and be done with him forever. Jesus took the old Adam on in his own body and said, "All right, do your worst. Put me to death and just see where it gets you." Then, just when the old Adam was leaning back, confident that by death he had destroyed Christ, Jesus was raised from the dead.

Christ's death and resurrection are the beginning of a new people, the birth of the new age. Christ is the *new* Adam, the "pioneer and perfecter of our faith," as Hebrews calls him (12:2). He is the only one who kept the First Commandment completely, counting on God to deliver him and give him everything good, even into the grave. He is the only one who gave himself for his neighbors completely, for us. Now God has raised him from the dead, the first one who is what Adam and Eve were made to be. Now he is at work to make you and all of his people what he is: completely new.

The old Adam dies and the new you comes forth each time that you hear this word, the word of Christ's cross and resurrection. It is the word of freedom for you—"freedom from sin, death and the power of the devil," as the explanation says. When Christ speaks it to you, he sets you free to be, to be what God made you to be.

As long as the old Adam lives, he tries to make it seem that God is your enemy—some kind of faraway judge you either have to ignore completely or appease by doing good things. Then you play God yourself, pretending you have to take care of yourself, worrying about whether you're going to get what you want and need.

Changes come

But when you hear Christ's word, that changes. For then you know that God is not your enemy, but your Father—the one who in Christ has given himself completely for you, withholding nothing. As you hear this the old Adam dies and you can say, "That's it. I repent. I don't want to be my own god anymore. I want you to be my God, and keep your promises to me."

When this happens, you know what the name "God" means at last, who he is, and what kind of God he is. You know that he is the Lord, who will give you everything good, come what may— that he is the God who doesn't hold out or hold back. And then you can speak to him as Jesus did, calling him "Abba! Father!"— not only "God the Father almighty," but "Dad" or "Papa." For he is your God, your heavenly "Dad," who comes as close to you —even closer—than your own parents.

Your neighbors change, too, as you hear Christ's word. As long as the old Adam is alive and kicking in you, he makes your neighbors seem like competitors or rivals to you. They are either so unimportant that you could care less about them, or they become so terribly important to you that you worry and wonder always about what they think of you.

But as you hear Christ's word, your neighbors become neighbors again, real neighbors. They are Christ's friends and yours—people you can help, care for, and enjoy; people who will help, care for, and enjoy you.

Christ's word changes the earth for you, too. To the old Adam the earth is a dump full of "resources" and "raw materials" he can take, use and exploit to satisfy himself. But as Christ makes you new with his word, the earth becomes God's garden for you. The land, the trees, the sky, the plants, and animals become gifts to you—gifts to love, to cherish, to protect and care for as God's own.

That's what Adam and Eve were made for—in Christ, that's what the new you is going to be: one who takes God at his word, who loves the neighbor and cares for the earth.

But now the old Adam doesn't just drop dead. As long as we live, he keeps struggling for little resurrections of his own, trying to take over again. He threatens us with our own deaths, trying to make it appear that dying is all we have to look forward to. And he tempts us in every way possible, working to replace confidence in God with doubt, love of the neighbor with animosity, and care of the earth with disregard for it. Wherever and whenever he succeeds, there is fear and doubt, worry and struggle and defeat.

The old Adam's number is up, though. As Christ defeated him with his cross and resurrection, he defeats the old Adam now with his word. And he is going before us into the future to establish his kingdom and bring in the new day. Then the old Adam will be dead forever, and we will all be new.

In the meantime, hearing Christ's word and awaiting his new day is like playing in the last part of a game that has already been won. The old Adam can do some damage and score some points. But he is bound to lose. For Christ has defeated him and will defeat him. And he has sent his Spirit to us to uphold, comfort and strengthen us, making us what he will be.

Chapter 15
God the Verb

THE THIRD ARTICLE

I believe in the Holy Ghost; the holy Christian church, the communion of saints; the forgiveness of sins; the resurrection of the body; and the life everlasting. Amen.

What does this mean?

I believe that I cannot by my own understanding or effort believe in Jesus Christ my Lord, or come to him. But the Holy Spirit has called me through the gospel, enlightened me with his gifts, and sanctified and kept me in true faith. In the same way he calls, gathers, enlightens, and sanctifies the whole Christian church on earth, and keeps it united with Jesus Christ in the one true faith. In this Christian church day after day he fully forgives my sins and the sins of all believers. On the last day he will raise me and all the dead and give me and all believers in Christ eternal life. This is most certainly true.

When the old Adam gets religion, one of his favorite tricks is trying to turn the Creed into a do-it-yourself kit. Right here, at the beginning of the Third Article, is where he strikes.

"Oh yes," the old Adam will say, "God supplies all the parts. He created you and he sent Jesus. But now you have to put the pieces together and finish the job. You have to accept him, you must believe in him, and do something to show you're sincere."

Like all of the old Adam's tricks, this sounds reasonable. But like all of his tricks, too, it has one purpose: to tie us up in ourselves.

When he springs it, the old Adam uses this trick to convince us that we can do everything God wants by our own efforts. Then we become proud and look down on our neighbors who, we conclude, aren't doing as well as we are.

Or, if that fails, the old Adam springs it another way to convince us that God won't have anything to do with us because we don't seem to be able to believe. Then we wind up despairing and hopeless, ready to give up. Either way, the joy of God's promise is destroyed.

That's why the explanation of the Third Article begins on what appears to be the wrong foot: "I believe that I cannot by my own understanding or effort believe in Jesus Christ my Lord, or come to him." The old you doesn't like to hear things like this, but it's said for a purpose: It is to stop the old Adam in his tracks, to close the door on this trick, and to point to the gifts God gives.

It is a fact that we cannot believe on our own, "by our own understanding or effort." But God doesn't expect us to. He doesn't have any time for do-it-yourself kits, not where his word and promise are concerned. When he starts a job, he finishes it. When he makes his gifts, he follows through on them, not only making them available but opening us up to receive them.

That's why God has sent us his Holy Spirit. It's the Spirit who brings us God's gifts. He works with the word in and through the church to make us what God intends us to be, his new people. What the old Adam wants to do alone, for himself, God insists on doing for us. That's the Spirit's work—to make us what God created us to be.

This may be hard to understand. Who is this Spirit? And what does he do? We'll discuss these questions in this chapter. Then, in the chapter that follows, we'll talk about where the Spirit works and what he's making of us.

The Spirit of life

One of the things that makes the Spirit sound so mysterious is his names. When he is called the Holy Spirit or the Holy Ghost, it can almost sound as if he is some kind of mist, or supernatural gas, or a super-ghost that blows around the atmosphere doing strange things.

That's something else that makes the Holy Spirit sound mysterious. He is given credit for all kinds of strange happenings, everything from speaking in tongues to little miracles.

The one who can clear up this mystery is Jesus. He promised the Spirit to his disciples, and to the church, before he was crucified. He called the Spirit the "Counselor." "And I will pray the Father," Jesus said, "and he will give you another Counselor, to be with you forever, even the Spirit of truth" (John 14:16-17). ". . . He will teach you all things, and bring to your remembrance all that I have said to you" (John 14:26). "But when the Counselor comes, whom I shall send to you from the Father, even the Spirit of truth, who proceeds from the Father, he will bear witness to me . . ." (John 15:26).

Jesus kept his promise, sending the Spirit to his disciples on the day of Pentecost, according to Luke. You probably remember the story—the "sound from heaven like the rush of a mighty wind," the "tongues of fire distributed and resting on them" (Acts 2:2-3). The gift of the Spirit changed everything for the disciples. When they received it, they started speaking in other languages and set out to tell everyone who would listen the story of Jesus' death and resurrection.

Who is the Spirit, then? He's the one who makes the story of Jesus known to us, who tells us of Christ and gives us his gifts. He is called a spirit or ghost because he is invisible, but he's not just any spirit or a ghost such as you've heard about in stories. He is God's Spirit, the Holy Spirit, the Spirit of life.

The Spirit was there when God created the heavens and the earth, "moving over the face of the waters," as Genesis says (1:2). He was there when God "formed man of dust from the ground and breathed into his nostrils the breath of life" (Gen. 2:7). He was there when Jesus was baptized. Jesus "saw the heavens opened and the Spirit descending on him like a dove," Mark says (1:10).

The Spirit is no afterthought. He is God himself, God being himself for us again, to make himself known to us. He is the Spirit of the risen Christ. He is the "Lord and giver of life," as the Nicene Creed calls him. He is God at work to give us life in Christ, making us what we are going to be.

The verb

Do you know the difference between nouns and verbs? You probably don't need another English lesson here, but the difference will tell you something more about the Holy Spirit. Nouns, like "chair," sit still—they name things, telling you what they are. Verbs, like "move" or "jump," never sit still, at least not for long. They are action words—even the quiet ones are always moving, acting, lively.

The Spirit is like a verb. Nouns don't work so well for him. He is always at work, always moving, active, making words jump and come to life. Knowing what he does, then, will tell you some more about who he is.

That's why the explanation of the Spirit's work in the Catechism is so full of verbs. The whole explanation is alive with them. What does the Spirit do? He *calls*, he *gathers*, he *enlightens*, he *sanctifies*.

First of all, the Spirit *calls*. That's what you do when you want to talk with your friends or get together with someone. You call them, whether it's on the telephone or by shouting across the street, giving them the words that you want to speak with them.

The Spirit calls in the same way—with his Word, the story of Jesus. He calls you through the Gospel.

The Spirit first called you when you were baptized, when you first heard the word of Christ's death and resurrection. He was sent to you at your Baptism, to call you and make you his. He knows your name, he calls you by name, and he keeps right on calling you, day after day. He calls relentlessly in the preaching of the word and the giving of the sacraments. He comes right out in the open, as he did at your Baptism, taking whatever risks he needs to take to give you the absolute gift. He holds nothing back. He simply says, "You are mine." That is his call.

But the Spirit never calls us alone. He is always *gathering* us together with other people. When you were baptized, more than likely your parents and some sponsors or some friends stood with you. As you have heard the word preached, you have been in the company of others—your family, a whole congregation of people. As you have gone to church school, it has been in groups.

That's how the Spirit gathers. He doesn't make lone rangers who travel by themselves. When he says, "You are mine," he says it to each of us, individually. But at the same time, he says it to all of us: "You are all mine." He puts us together with others, making us a part of them and them a part of us. That is the church—a people gathered together to hear the word and receive the sacraments, a people called and gathered by the Spirit.

Having called and gathered you together with others, the Holy Spirit *enlightens* you. To enlighten something means to turn the lights on it, to light up what has been dark, to make sense out of what has been puzzling, to clear up what has been mysterious.

The Spirit has enlightened you in the same way as he has called you and gathered you together with others: with his word. He has enlightened you through preaching, in Sunday school classes, at home having devotions. He is enlightening you now, according to Jesus' promise, using words that tell of Christ and what he does.

When the Spirit enlightens, though, he doesn't stop with understanding. He will bring you to the point where you can say, "So that's who he is. So that's the way he works." But beyond that, he will bring you to the point where you can say, "That's for me. I want his word and promise." As that happens, he's got you on your way to becoming what God made

you to be. He will keep enlightening you too, lighting up more and more for you as he brings out the new you.

That brings us to one more verb: the Spirit *sanctifies*. It is a church word, one that you don't hear very often on the street or in school. It comes from an old Latin word that means "sacred" or "holy." And it sums up, in a word, everything the Spirit does, his whole purpose for us. He is making us holy. That means he is making us what God made us to be, his new people.

How is the Spirit doing this? Where does he work, and what are we going to be like when he makes us holy? Those questions will have to wait until the next chapter.

In the meantime, though, we know who is doing this job and what he's doing. The old Adam likes to think that you can make a believer out of yourself, that you're the one who has to make yourself what God wants you to be. It can't be done. Having created us and come to us in Christ, God sends his Spirit to give us all of his gifts. He's the one who calls us, gathers us, enlightens and sanctifies us. He's the one who is making us what Adam and Eve were made to be.

Chapter 16

Saints and Sinners

If you were to pick out a word to describe yourself, it probably wouldn't be "holy." You probably wouldn't call yourself a "saint," either. Whether out of fear of seeming too proud or out of knowledge of our own shortcomings, we usually don't use these words to speak of ourselves.

You might not choose these words to describe the church, either. The Creed uses them, speaking of "the holy Christian church, the communion of saints." But the Creed doesn't have eyes or ears to see what happens in the church or to hear about it later. If the conduct of the people in it is a measure of what it means to be holy, Christian, and saintly, the church might have a hard time qualifying.

But even if they aren't words you'd choose, they describe what the Holy Spirit is making of you, and what the church is. He is making you holy, what God made you to be. And he is doing it through the Word he speaks in "the holy Christian church," which is "the communion of saints."

Last chapter we discussed who the Spirit is and what he does. He is the Spirit of life, the Holy Spirit, God being himself for us again to call, gather, enlighten, and sanctify us as his own.

Now, in this chapter, having seen who does the work and what he's doing, we're going to take a look at his workshop, his tools, and what he's making of us—holy people. The Spirit's workshop is the church. As he works in and through the church with his tools, the word and the sacraments, the church is made the "communion of saints" and we are made holy."

The Spirit's workshop

It may seem like more of the old Adam's bragging to say that God's own Spirit is at work in the church. It doesn't take much to see that the church isn't perfect—far from it.

The church has all the faults and problems of the people who belong to it. It can be boring and routine. It can be clubby, cliquey, and downright nasty at times. The church has pretenders in it who think they're going to get to heaven by being more religious than others. And it has plenty of people who say one thing on Sunday morning and do something far different during the week.

If it depended on people, on what we say and do, to make the church what it is, it would never be holy, Christian, or a communion of saints.

But with all of our shortcomings and failings, Christ has promised that the Spirit will speak to us. "When the Counselor comes," he said, "whom I shall send to you from the Father . . . he will bear witness to me" (John 15:26). It is the Spirit's speaking, his making Christ known to us, that makes the church what it is: the people of God gathered together to hear the word and receive the sacraments.

Last chapter we discussed how the Spirit calls and gathers us. Beginning in the sacrament of Baptism, he calls us again and again through the word of Christ, saying "You are mine." And as he calls us, he never leaves us alone. He keeps putting us in the company of other people, making us a part of them and them a part of us.

The Spirit calls and gathers throughout the world. Wherever he goes, the Spirit sets people apart for himself and brings them together with others. Though there are many small gatherings of many different kinds in many different places, there is one church. It is called the "catholic" or universal church, because it is made up of all the people the Spirit has called and gathered throughout the world: Lutherans and Roman Catholics, Presbyterians and Methodists, Christians of every shape, size, and color.

113

This gathering of people called by the Spirit, whether in a small congregation or the worldwide gathering, is the first mark of the church.

To call and gather us, and to enlighten and sanctify us, the Spirit uses his tools: the word and the sacraments. They are the second mark of the church, and the most important one. For it's through them that the Spirit does his speaking and gives his gifts.

The Spirit speaks to us by making his word fit for the lips of common, ordinary, everyday people—people like your pastor, your father or mother or guardians, your Sunday school teacher or catechist. As they tell you of Christ, the Spirit is at work in the word to tell you that you are his. Wherever the Spirit goes, God's word is spoken. And wherever God's word is spoken, the Spirit is at work in it.

With the word, the Spirit also uses the sacraments—Baptism and the Lord's Supper. Through them, as you will see in later chapters, he gives us Christ's gifts to make us his.

That's why the church is called holy, Christian, and the communion of saints. It's not because the building is any different. Nor is it because the people in your church or you yourself are so much better than others, either.

The church is holy because the Spirit is holy and he's the one who makes the church. The church is Christian because in and through it, the Spirit works throughout the world to make Christ

known and to give his gifts. And it is the communion of saints because it is the gathering of people who have been called by the Spirit and who are being made saints through the word and the sacraments.

God's saints

But now what about you? How can you be called holy or a saint? What is the Spirit making of you and the rest of us he has called?

You are called both holy and a saint because the word the Spirit speaks to you in the church is Christ's word of forgiveness. It is pronounced each Sunday in your congregation, and can be spoken to you any time you want to hear it. "Almighty God, our heavenly Father, hath had mercy upon us, and hath given his only Son to die for us, and for his sake forgiveth us all our sins," the pastor says.

As these words are spoken, you can be sure that the Spirit is with you to give you exactly what they say. He is the Spirit of the risen Christ, the friend of sinners. When he says, "You are mine. I forgive you," all of your sin is wiped out completely. He doesn't just overlook it or say that it doesn't matter. He destroys it, erases it entirely, so that there is nothing left of it. All that you have done and failed to do is forgiven.

When you hear these words, then, you can be sure that God is making you as innocent as Adam and Eve were before their rebellion. God has decided for you—he is holding nothing against you. You are holy, one of his saints.

The Spirit goes even further. He not only tells you what Christ has done about your past, forgiving you all your sins. He tells you what Christ is doing about your future—that he is going to raise you from the dead.

This word is spoken to you each Sunday, too, and in the same part of the service: the absolution. "To them that believe on his Name," the pastor says, "he (God) giveth power to become the sons of God, and bestoweth upon them his Holy Spirit. He that believeth and is baptized, shall be saved."

Hearing this promise, again you can be sure that God will do just what he says—that "on the last day he will raise you and all the dead and give you and all believers in Christ eternal life."

115

He's not just going to raise part of you from the dead—the part of you that is like everyone else. He's going to raise you, the real you, the whole you, the person you are. It will be "the resurrection of the body," as the Creed says, and you will be with him forever. For he has decided that you are one of his saints, and declared you so, giving you his word that he is going to raise you.

Now doesn't that change everything? You don't have to try to cover up where you've been wrong or failed to do right. You don't have to prove that you're holier or better than anyone else. God has forgiven you, and he will forgive you.

You don't have to be anxious, either—worrying, wondering, trying to "be like God." He has promised to raise you from the dead, to take you to himself as his very own.

Now, as you hear the Spirit's word and promise, you can be what God intends you to be, the person he made you to be, one of his new creatures. Taking God at his word, you can rely on him for everything good, fearing, loving, and trusting him above all things. Taking him at his word, you can be a neighbor, enjoying and helping the people you live and go to school and work with. Taking God at his word, you can help to care for the earth, too, enjoying and cherishing it as his precious gift.

That's what the Spirit is making of you: a believer. He's not making people who will keep trying to be somebody else, who pretend to be something they're not. He's not making people with the pinched-up faces and the knowing sneer of the self-satisfied,

outwardly pious, either. He's making holy people, believers—laughing, loving, singing, praising, grateful people who are what God has made us to be.

It's not always so easy to believe, though, is it? Maybe you've known some times when it hasn't been difficult—some times when worries have disappeared, when you have been sure that God was caring for you, when you've enjoyed your neighbors and God's creation.

But you've also known some other kinds of times, perhaps—times when questions and doubts have made it difficult to believe; times when your neighbors have seemed more like enemies than friends; times when the creation has seemed pretty hostile or you haven't cared the slightest bit about it.

You are not yet what God made you to be. There are two yous, an old one and a new one: an old you that struggles and fights, worries, and wonders, because it is going to die, and a new you born in the water and the word of Baptism. These two yous fight within you, within each of us, and they will keep on struggling until the old you, the old Adam, finally dies forever—when we die.

But in that struggle now, you know the promises of the Creed. You know that God the Father almighty, the Maker of heaven and earth, is your Father; that Jesus Christ, his only Son, our Lord, has taken your sin and death upon himself, becoming your friend; that the Holy Spirit is at work right now, in and through the church, speaking the word of forgiveness and the promise of the resurrection to you.

Knowing that, hearing God's promise, you can be sure that the old Adam is going to lose, and not only lose, but die. In all of your struggles, fears and doubts, the Spirit is at work to make a believer out of you. And as he does, he'll keep you, too, never letting you go. You are his. And someday, when the last day comes, there will no longer be two yous but one: the new you he has made.

Chapter 17

He Puts the Words in Our Mouths

THE INTRODUCTION

Our Father who art in heaven.

What does this mean?

Here God encourages us to believe that he is
truly our Father and that we are his children.
We therefore are to pray to him with complete
confidence just as children speak
to their loving father.

THE DOXOLOGY

**For thine is the kingdom and the power
and the glory forever and ever. Amen.**

What does "Amen" mean?

Amen means *Yes, it shall be so.*
We say *Amen* because we are certain that
such petitions are pleasing to our Father in heaven
and are heard by him. For he himself has commanded
us to pray in this way and has promised to hear us.

Luther once called the Lord's Prayer "the greatest martyr on earth." Writing to a barber who had asked for help with his prayers, Luther went on to explain that it is such a martyr because "everybody tortures and abuses it while few comfort and cheer it with proper use."

It's as true now as it was in Luther's day. The Lord's Prayer is the best-known prayer in the church. But it is seldom prayed with all of the joy, confidence, and certainty that is in it.

Part of the problem is that it's so familiar. Knowing the words so well, it is easy to say them without thinking—as automatically as you jump when you hear a loud noise. Nobody wants to pray in this way, but it gets to be a reflex or habit. And trying to change it, to pray it more meaningfully, can be awfully frustrating.

There's a more serious problem, too. For many people, not only the Lord's Prayer, but every kind of praying has lost its edge. It sometimes seems that nobody is listening when we pray, that prayer is a pious exercise or a religious way of talking to ourselves. When this happens, the Lord's Prayer hardly seems like a person-to-person talk with our Father. Rather, it is pointless, meaningless—nothing more than a polite way to start or end meetings, services, or classes at the church.

These are some good reasons for taking a careful look at the Lord's Prayer. We'll start out by looking at the beginning and the end of it to see how it can be prayed with confidence and certainty. Then we'll look some more at how we can call God *Father*, even when the old Adam makes such a mess of our prayers. Hopefully, in this chapter and those that follow, you'll see why the Lord's Prayer has been called a summary of the whole gospel, of all God's promises.

Praying for certain

In the Commandments and the Creed, God has already shown us how we can be certain that he hears our prayers. He not only hears them—he wants us to pray, teaches us to pray, and prays for us.

First of all, we can pray because God has promised to be our God. It's the First Commandment again—"I am the Lord your

God. You shall have no other gods before me." "I am yours," God says, "and you are mine."

In Christ, God put this promise into action. He made it flesh and blood for us, becoming a person like us to become our friend and Lord. He went to the cross and death for us, bearing our sins in his body, to carry out the promise of the First Commandment—to make us his own people, his sons and daughters.

Because we have this promise in Christ, we can call on God for anything and everything we need. It is like getting word from the president or prime minister that says, "Call me when you need help." But it is on a far bigger scale, for it is God's word and promise. Because he is your God and promises to help you, you can say to the Creator of the heavens and the earth, "Father, you have promised—I need your help."

But second, God not only tells us that we may pray—he commands us to pray. It is as if he said to himself, "If I just tell them that they can pray, they might not dare to. I'll command them to pray so that they'll know how much I want them to come to me for whatever they need." Or it's like your mother, father or a friend saying, "Now listen. I want to help you—call me and I'll be right there."

So, in the Second Commandment, God tells us to "call upon him in prayer, praise and thanksgiving." It is a friendly command that God lovingly gives us to assure us that he wants us to pray.

God could hardly do more than that, we might think. "I've told you that you may pray," he could have said, "and not only that, I've commanded you to pray. If you mess it up now, it's all over."

But God did more. Having given us his promise and commanded us to pray, he himself teaches us how to pray. That's why it's called the *Lord's* Prayer. It is the prayer that Christ taught to his disciples and, through his word, teaches to us.

Perhaps the disciples had some of the same questions and problems many of us have with prayer. Maybe praying had become an automatic routine for them. Or maybe they weren't quite sure how to act or what to say when they prayed. Whatever the reason, they asked Jesus to teach them how to pray (Luke 11:1).

There are two versions of the Lord's Prayer. One is in Matthew 6:9-13 and the other is in Luke 11:2-4. We use the version found in Matthew. The doxology, "For thine is the kingdom and the power and the glory forever and ever" isn't in either Matthew or Luke but has been part of the Lord's Prayer ever since the first century.

The fact that it is Jesus who teaches us this prayer is most important. He is Emmanuel, God himself with us. When he teaches us to pray, he not only knows what he's talking about—he's the one we are praying to.

He is the one whose name we pray will be hallowed, the one whose kingdom will come and whose will will be done. He is the one who gives us our daily bread and forgives us our trespasses, who helps us in temptation and delivers us from evil.

So praying the Lord's Prayer is like singing in a choir or playing in a band directed by the one who wrote the music. Or it is like being coached by the one who invented the game and who will judge the outcome. Or it is like being given the answers by the one who will give you the test. Jesus, the one who hears our prayers and answers them, puts the words into our mouths to teach us to pray.

But God doesn't even stop there. "We do not know how to pray as we ought," Paul says in Romans 8:26. Even when Jesus puts the words in our mouths, our prayers easily become routine and meaningless. We worry and doubt, wondering if God really listens. Or we start thinking about how sincere we are and how God must be impressed with how much we want him to help us. No matter how hard we try, we can't pray as we should.

But God isn't waiting for us to make our prayers good enough for him. Having said that we may pray, having commanded us to pray and having taught us to pray, God himself prays with and for us. ". . . But the Spirit himself intercedes for us with sighs too deep for words," Paul says (Rom. 8:26). It's like a father or mother who helps a child in every way and finally says, "Here, I'll do that for you." Having said to each of us, "You are mine," God goes all the way for us, making us his own.

That's the basis for our confidence, and that's why we can pray with complete certainty that God hears us. We can pray to him as children speak to their loving parents, confidently and joyfully, because God promises that we may, commands us and teaches us to pray, and then prays with and for us.

Calling him Father
That's why we can call God *Father,* calling out to him as you call out to your mother or father at home: "Dad," or "Mom."

God became your Father when you were baptized, when he first promised to be your God. That was and is his promise to you. Not, "I'm going to be *like* a father," or *"like* a mother to you," but "I'm going to be your God"—your father and mother all wrapped up into one.

We can call God *Father,* too, because he is going to "dwell with us," as the book of Revelation says (21:3). He isn't going to be an absentee father who stays away, sending home occasional letters and gifts. He dwells with us now, in his word and the sacraments. And he will stay with us in the future, raising us from the dead to take us to himself. Then he will live with us as loving parents live with their children, and we will be with him.

The old Adam doesn't care for that. In fact, he hates it. Prayer is a big problem for him, something to be avoided or used only for your own purposes, because when you pray you are admitting that you need God's help and grace. That's the one thing the old Adam doesn't want to admit, not unless it's with the provision that you tell God exactly what to do and how to do it. So the old Adam makes the Lord's Prayer automatic and pointless, or else insists that God has to do his bidding.

But once you hear the promise in and behind it, the Lord's Prayer becomes entirely different. While he puts the old Adam to death in each of us, God calls out the new you—the you who can and will call on him with joy and certainty. As this new you comes forth, the you who is a believer, the Lord's Prayer blossoms and sings with all the love and grace of Gods' promise.

Then it's not dead repetition or some kind of hocus-pocus anymore, something that we just do out of habit. Rather, it is a person-to-person conversation with your God, the God of the promise, the God of Good Friday and Easter. Then, boldly and confidently, you can begin by saying "Our Father who art in heaven," and when you have finished praying, say *Amen*—that's the way it's going to be.

Chapter 18

Praying for Our Father

THE FIRST PETITION
Hallowed be thy name.

What does this mean?

God's name certainly is holy in itself, but we
ask in this prayer that we may keep it holy.

When does this happen?

God's name is hallowed whenever his Word is taught
in its truth and purity, and we as children of God
live in harmony with it. Help us to do this,
heavenly Father! But anyone who teaches or lives
contrary to the Word of God dishonors God's name
among us. Keep us from doing this, heavenly Father!

THE SECOND PETITION
Thy kingdom come.

What does this mean?

God's kingdom comes indeed without our praying
for it, but we ask in this prayer that it
may come also to us.

When does this happen?

God's kingdom comes when our heavenly Father gives
us his Holy Spirit, so that by his grace
we believe his holy Word and live a godly life
on earth now and in heaven forever.

One of the biggest surprises in the Lord's Prayer comes right at the beginning. In the first three petitions—the two above plus the one that will be considered in the next chapter—Jesus teaches us to pray *for* God. The last four petitions are more like what we would expect—in them we pray *to* God for our neighbors and ourselves.

In the first petitions, then, we're not only praying *to* God but *for* him—that *his* name will be hallowed and that *his* kingdom will come. Why?

There could be one easy explanation—if these petitions hadn't been taught to us by Jesus! Some might say that we're praying for God to butter him up a little bit—saying a few nice words about his name and his new day before getting down to what's really important, what we want or need.

But that's not the way the God of the promise—the God of the exodus, Good Friday, and Easter—operates. Not for a minute. He's no pompous swelled-head who keeps one hand on his treasure chest while holding out the other to be stroked with bribes. He is the God who promises, the God who raised Jesus from the dead, your heavenly Father who gives all that is his as a gift, without payment or price.

Why do we pray for him, then? Maybe if we look at what we're asking for, we'll get some clues. Then we'll come back to this question and see if we can't find an answer.

God's name and his goal

The introduction to the Lord's Prayer and the First Petition go together just like the first two commandments. In the commandments, after promising to be our God and giving us his name, God commands us to use his name rightly. The beginning of the Lord's Prayer follows the same order. After calling upon God as our Father in the introduction, we pray in the First Petition that his name will be hallowed.

Now "hallowed" isn't a common word. The Lord's Prayer is probably the only place where you use it. But if you take the Second Commandment as a clue, you should have a pretty good idea of what it means. When we pray "hallowed be thy name," we are asking God to give us what he commands in the Second Commandment—that he will bring out the new you in us who

125

will use his name as he intends it to be used, to "call upon him in prayer, praise, and thanksgiving."

That's just the opposite of what the old Adam wants. The old you in you is always wondering how you can make a name for yourself—a name people will respect, admire, and appreciate. To this old you, God's name is good for nothing. It is a name to be used to curse and swear, to lie and deceive, to conjure up magic, or to prove how religious you are. The old Adam's contempt for God's name is so deep and so wide that there is almost nothing more common than taking his name in vain.

As the new you that God calls out in Baptism takes shape, however, something different happens. Instead of using it as an exclamation point for curses and lies, the new you takes God's name as a great and precious gift. Because he has given you his name, you can call upon God, asking his help, praising him, and giving thanks for all of his promises and gifts. You know who he is, what kind of a God he is. He is the God who makes things out of nothing and raises the dead; the God of grace who speaks to you through his word to make you and all things new.

Hearing that, something else happens to the new you, too. Instead of being embarrassed or slightly ashamed to use God's name, the new you treats it as the name which is above every other name. It is the name to speak to others, telling all who will listen what God has done and promises to do. That's how God intends his name to be used. He gives it to us not only so that we can call upon him but so that we can speak of him to others.

The old Adam knows how to speak of God to others, too. When he goes religious, he makes the clouds echo with shouts of "praise God," "praise the Lord," and so on. But somehow when the old Adam gets ahold of the name, he always turns it around to point to himself. "Praise God" on the old Adam's lips means "Praise me, for I am so religious." "Praise the Lord" means "Look at me, and you'll see the genuine article."

The name properly used

So when we pray "hallowed be thy name," we're not only asking God to continue making a new you in us who will use his name properly—we're asking him to see to it that his name is used properly wherever it is spoken. His name is hallowed, then, "wherever his word is taught in its truth and purity, and we as children of God live in harmony with it." God's going to make that happen, calling out the new you in us and a new creation across the face of the universe that will hallow his name.

The Second Petition, "Thy kingdom come," fits in with the commandments, too. In the Third Commandment, God commands us to remember his day—not only the Sabbath day each week but the new day coming. In this petition, we pray for the new day, asking that God's kingdom will come.

127

The word "kingdom" probably isn't a part of your everyday language, either. It smacks of another age, the time of Lancelot or Prince Valiant, when there were kings and lords who ruled over little kingdoms of their own.

God's kingdom isn't a place, as those were. The church isn't his kingdom, either. God's kingdom is his rule or, to use another old word, his reign. God's kingdom comes wherever he rules. It will finally come when he establishes his rule over all the earth and makes all things new.

God has begun to establish his rule over you already. He started in your Baptism, when he sent his Spirit to begin making the new you in you. He has been at work since—calling you, gathering you with others, enlightening you, sanctifying you.

But God's kingdom hasn't come finally, yet. God has a rival in you—the old you. And though they are not nearly as powerful as he is, God has rivals across the face of the earth, "powers and principalities," as Paul calls them in Ephesians 6:12. When God's kingdom finally comes, he will destroy all of his rivals. Then there will be no more old Adam in you that fights and struggles against the new you. You will be wholly and completely God's. And then there will be no more rivals who fill the earth with sin and death. The creation will be new—God's own creation, the new creation.

So, in the second petition, we are praying for the new you and the new day. When we pray, "Thy kingdom come," we are asking God to establish his rule over us and to keep his promise, bringing in his rule or reign over all the earth. That is his goal—to make us and all things new. And that's what he's going to do.

Praying for God

Have you seen enough clues now to answer that first question, why Jesus teaches us to pray *for* God?

The first clue is in Luther's explanations to these petitions. We're not praying for God because he somehow needs help, ours or anyone else's. "God's name certainly is holy in itself"—he doesn't need our prayers or our help to make it holy. "God's kingdom comes indeed without our prayer"—he doesn't have to wait for us to pray to help him make his kingdom come.

128

"All right," the old Adam says, "if that's the case, why bother to pray these petitions at all? If God can get along without me, why should I bother my head about his name and his kingdom?" The old Adam always likes to make it sound as if he's doing God a favor. He's the old you who thinks you can "allow" God to do something, "letting him do whatever he wants," as if God were some poor, helpless beggar who had to come and ask for your permisson before he could do what he wants.

That's not the way it works. God doesn't need permission from us for anything. He doesn't need our prayers or occasional good deeds, either. He doesn't depend on us—we depend on him.

Why do we pray these petitions, then? In both of these petitions, we are praying not only for God but for ourselves, that his name will be hallowed "among us" and that his kingdom will come "also to us."

Does that sound complicated? Think of your school's basketball or hockey team. If you don't play for the team, there's nothing you can do to help them win. When the whistle blows, all you can do is sit and watch or stand and cheer.

But still you hope, and maybe pray, too, that they will have a good game, that they will be respected, appreciated, and admired. And you hope and maybe even pray, too, that they will "establish their rule" over all the teams, defeating every rival and taking home the championship.

If they get a good reputation and win their games, the team members get some benefits for themselves. But you benefit from it too, otherwise you wouldn't feel bad if they lost.

Now, God doesn't hold pep meetings or organize cheering sections with pastors for cheerleaders. Furthermore, there's no doubt about him winning the game. He's going to win it, hands down.

But still we pray, as Jesus taught us to pray, "hallowed be thy name," and "thy kingdom come." We pray for God because we love him and want his name to be used as he intends it to be used, and because we want his kingdom to come. But while we pray for him, we are also praying for ourselves—asking that he will help us to speak his name and his word in all their truth and purity, asking him to keep his word that he will include us in his victory.

Chapter 19

Victory Is Certain

THE THIRD PETITION
Thy will be done on earth as it is in heaven.

What does this mean?
The good and gracious will of God is surely done
without our prayer, but we ask in this prayer that
it may be done also among us.

When does this happen?
God's will is done when he hinders and defeats every
evil scheme and purpose of the devil, the world,
and our sinful self, which would prevent us from
keeping his name holy and would oppose the coming of
his kingdom. And his will is done when he strengthens
our faith and keeps us firm in his Word as long as
we live. This is his gracious and good will.

There are two sides to this petition just as there are two sides
to every person's story, including your own. On the one side this
petition is full of certainty. "The good and gracious will of God
is surely done without prayer." Because God is God, he's going
to have his way, no matter what.

But then there's the other side: "but we ask in this prayer that it may be done also among us." Is that for certain, too? Sometimes it doesn't seem very certain at all. For wherever God's word and promise are heard, there is bound to be opposition and plenty of it.

Maybe you've seen the same two sides in your own story. On the one side, God has made his decision about you, promising to be your God and give you everything good. You have received all kinds of gifts from him, too. That is certain.

But on the other side, maybe you haven't been able to see good in everything that has happened to you. Maybe you have had some times of uncertainty and doubt about God's promises or about yourself. Maybe, after looking around, you've seen some things that make you wonder who is really in charge in the world—if it's God or some unknown, unseen power that rules by chance and luck. Maybe, in fact, you've sometimes wondered if this whole business about God and his promises isn't a myth—a nice idea that sounds good but doesn't really mean much.

These two sides to your own story and the stories of all God's people are the special concern of the Third Petition. As we pray "thy will be done, on earth as it is in heaven," we are asking God to put the two sides together—to give us the certainty of his promise in the midst of the opposition, pain, and trouble that we know.

So, in this chapter, we'll consider two things: first, the other side of the story, some of the opposition we see; and second, what God does with this opposition.

The opponents

It's easy to suppose that living in God's promises ought to be like cruising down a freeway through the wide open spaces on a beautiful summer afternoon. If we were, you wouldn't have to worry about anything like traffic, fog, intersections, possible accidents, or breakdowns along the way.

But that's not the way it works, not if what happened to Jesus, Peter, Paul, the prophets before them, and Christians since is any indication. Wherever the gospel goes, it makes people new, giving freedom from the past and hope for the future. But wherever it goes it also meets opposition. In fact, the more the gospel is proclaimed and heard, the more it is fought.

You know what happened to Jesus. If anyone could have expected a cruising, easy time of it it should have been Jesus. He was and is God's own beloved son, after all.

But there were two sides to his story, too. As he proclaimed God's promise and went to work with it, some heard and believed. But others, including his own disciples, doubted. And still others met him with the most fearsome opposition, until finally he was crucified.

"Remember the word that I said to you," Jesus told his disciples when he was leaving them, "'A servant is not greater than his master.' If they persecuted me, they will persecute you" (John 15:20). "In the world you will have tribulation," he said (16:33). That's the way it works. Just as Jesus met a ready welcome from some and was condemned by others, today his word is heard by some and opposed by others.

Who are these opponents? Luther lists three of them in his explanation of the petition. They are our sinful self, the world, and the devil.

By now you are familiar with the first opponent. "Our sinful self" is the old you, the old Adam in you and each of us. While piously praying "thy will be done," the old Adam's deepest wish is just the opposite: "*my* will be done." That's where the conflict centers. Whenever you hear God's word and promise, the old you fights it. And he continues to fight it as long as you live, no matter how hard you struggle against him.

The old Adam's stock-in-trade is trying to make it look as if you're in charge of things while God is some kind of super–servant who takes your orders. To this end, the old Adam plots and schemes, sometimes coming straight out with unbelief or indifference to the promise, at other times trying to make you look religious while holding out for your own way.

Though you may not have thought of it this way, the second opponent is familiar to you, too. It is the world. You're not the only one with the old Adam in you—all of us have this old you in us—every living human being. So we don't just resist the promises of God alone—we have a world of company.

The world's creed has three articles: good luck, hard work, and getting ahead. In the first article it makes it appear that everything happens by luck. If you get something you've wanted, it's because you're lucky. If you don't, you're unlucky.

But sometimes it takes more than luck. So the world's creed has a second article: hard work. If people will only knuckle down and put their minds to it, the world says, they'll be able to do whatever they want. The third article is the goal: getting ahead, ahead of what you've gotten so far, ahead of your neighbors, ahead of whoever gets in your way.

So the world resists the gospel. It is too busy looking for luck, working hard, getting ahead, to have any time for promises. Either that or it wants promises that work like coupons—you turn them in someplace and get ahead some more. It's not a joke—perhaps you've tasted some of the ridicule that sometimes comes from other people when they hear you have ears for the promise. That's just the beginning.

The third opponent of the gospel is the devil. To the old Adam and the world, the suggestion that there might actually be a devil seems ridiculous. Because the old Adam keeps insisting that you can take charge of everything that happens to you, he doesn't want you thinking that there is anything like a powerful force of evil around that might be stronger than you are.

People who have wrestled with the promise know something different, though: that no matter how hard we struggle, hope, and pray for faith, something stronger than us seems to be fighting against us. That's the devil's specialty.

Luther used to call him "God's ape," God's mimic. The devil makes himself look like God, imitating him to destroy faith. So wherever the devil goes, he leaves footprints full of doubt, despair, anxiety, and agony. Either that, or he lulls people to sleep with his imitations, making them imagine that they are secure and need not be bothered with God's promise.

Though they are nowhere near as powerful as God is, with three opponents like these hard at work it's no wonder the world is so full of pain, struggle, and death. It's not surprising either that God's opponents would like to pin the blame on him for the suffering they cause in the creation.

Hindering and strengthening

What do you suppose God does with these opponents? You can be sure that he is not going to sit in heaven twiddling his thumbs. His will is to bring out the new you in us and to bring in his new creation, his kingdom. So God fights the opponents of his promise in two ways: he "hinders and defeats every evil scheme and purpose" they come with, and he "strengthens our faith and keeps us firm in his word as long as we live."

God uses several means to hinder and defeat the old Adam and his partners. First of all, he uses the commandments to pen them up or keep them on leashes, putting them under controls that keep them from going too far. In this way, he keeps order in the creation and protects each of us.

Then, while he keeps order, God takes away the opponents' weapons and uses them against them. For instance, one of the devil's favorite weapons is death. He'll wave it in front of you saying, "What difference does it make—you're going to die any-way," and so try to frighten you into thinking that nothing matters but trying to grab as much as you can while you can.

But then God takes hold of the weapon the devil is using and turns it on him. "Yes," God says to you, "you are going to die. It's not going to be any fun, either. But here is my promise: I am going to raise you from the dead."

In this way, God uses the fright and worry the devil has caused in you to show you how great and gracious his own promises are. Luther called this God's "strange work." What the old Adam, the world, and the devil use to drive you *from* the promise—such as suffering, pain, and death—God uses to drive you *to* the promise.

But God doesn't just fight his opponents from a distance. In Christ, he has taken them on himself, doing battle with his enemies to bring them to their knees and put them to death. Now they die each time that you hear Christ's word and promise. On the last day, God will put them to death forever. That's the goal that God has set for us and his whole creation—to destroy all of his enemies and make all things new.

In the meantime, while he hinders and defeats his enemies, God also encourages us by strengthening our faith and keeping us firm in his word. He does this through his Spirit, who works in the word and the sacraments. Day after day he speaks to us, telling us all what he has done and will do to make us his own.

Having given us his word at our Baptism that he will be our God, he also comes to be with us in the Lord's Supper, renewing us, strengthening us, giving us hope and courage. Through it all, he surrounds us with other people who will help and care for us. Above all, he himself works, day and night, to keep us in faith.

There are two sides to your story, just as there are two sides to Jesus' story and two sides to everyone's story. So we all pray, "thy will be done, on earth as it is in heaven," asking that God will give us the certainty that his will "may be done also among us." He will give us that certainty because he has promised to, and he keeps his word.

Chapter 20

Every Day a Gift

THE FOURTH PETITION
Give us this day our daily bread.

What does this mean?
God gives daily bread, even without our prayer, to
all people, though sinful, but we ask in this prayer
that he will help us to realize this and to receive
our daily bread with thanks.

What is meant by daily bread?
Daily bread includes everything needed for this life,
such as food and clothing, home and property, work
and income, a devoted family, an orderly community,
good government, favorable weather, peace and health,
a good name, and true friends and neighbors.

THE FIFTH PETITION
**And forgive us our trespasses, as we forgive
those who trespass against us.**

What does this mean?
We ask in this prayer that our Father in heaven
would not hold our sins against us and because of
them refuse to hear our prayer. And we pray that he
would give us everything by grace, for we sin every
day and deserve nothing but punishment. So we on
our part will heartily forgive and gladly do good
to those who sin against us.

After praying for the great and glorious gifts of God—his name, his kingdom, and his will—now we get down to the basic stuff of daily life, bread and butter and getting along with our neighbors.

To be sure, the first three petitions have plenty to do with daily life, too. As God creates the new you in us who will hallow his name, he charges our days with freedom. And as he helps us to look forward to the coming of his kingdom, he fills our days with hope, giving us the whole new creation to look forward to.

But freedom and hope for the new day wouldn't be complete if our tables were empty. They wouldn't be complete if we had to wonder constantly what God and our neighbors think of us, either. So, after teaching us to pray for the new you and the new creation he has promised, Jesus tells us to ask for daily bread and forgiveness as well.

It's not that we somehow have to talk God into giving us these gifts. He has given us plenty of daily bread already, probably more than our share. And over and over again, he has assured us that he forgives us. He will continue to give us these gifts, too, along with everything else we need to live while we await his new day. That's his promise—the promise of the First Commandment and all three articles of the Creed.

The trouble is that we don't always realize it. In fact, we seldom do. We either take daily bread and forgiveness for granted, never giving them a thought, or we worry ourselves sick about them, thinking that somehow God will forget us. So Jesus teaches us to pray for these gifts, helping us in this way to realize who gives them to us.

Why is it so hard to realize that these are gifts? That's the first question we'll consider this chapter. After that, we'll discuss what realizing the gifts can mean for daily life.

Looking to ourselves

If there's one thing your neighbors have in common with you, it is worrying. They might be taller or shorter, fatter or skinnier, better or worse; they might be neighbors across the street, across the border, or across the ocean, but you can be sure that they worry just like you do. Worrying seems to be one common denominator that marks us all as people.

138

Sometimes there seems to be very good reason for worry. To put bread on our tables, for instance, it takes a whole combination of people and things working together. It takes good farmers, good farms, good crops, good prices, good stores, good jobs to earn good money.

Food isn't all we need to live each day, either. We also need clothing, places to live, good governments to protect us, good names and good neighbors, plus more. And each requires its own combination, just like food, of people and things working together.

With so many needs and so many combinations needed to get them, it isn't any wonder that people worry. You may not have gone to bed hungry once in your life. But many people do and with the old Adam and the devil hard at work, there's no guarantee that you won't sometime be one of them. That can be worrisome.

If you haven't yet had to worry about the food on your table or the other things you need for your body, you've probably done quite a bit of worrying about what other people think of you. That, too, seems to be one of our characteristics as people—feeling out of step or out of place with the people around us, feeling guilty. Some notice it more, some less, but the feeling always seem to be there somewhere, gnawing its way around.

Here again there may seem to be good reason for it. You might have done something that makes you feel guilty in the eyes of others. Or you might just feel there is something about you that makes you less than acceptable, less than desirable—whether it's as small as an unsightly wart or as big as feeling awkward, ugly, or stupid.

If that isn't enough, there can be some deeper worries. No matter how often we hear God's promise of forgiveness, at times it is easy to become convinced that we have done things to disqualify ourselves from it—that we're out of place or out of step not only with some neighbors, but with God himself. At such times, people can try as hard as they want to not to worry about it, but the feeling keeps coming back.

It is these worries about what we need to live and what others think of us that make it so difficult to realize that God gives us everything we need as a gift. They are the old Adam's worries. That's how the old Adam, the world, and the devil work—by focusing our attention on what we love or fear and making it appear that we have to get or avoid those things by ourselves. Then we worry.

See how it works? As long as we're worried, we keep looking to ourselves, trying to find ways to get what we want or to avoid what we fear. Then if we get enough food and get along well with others, we take such gifts for granted, and start worrying about something else we want or fear. Or if we're hungry and feeling guilty, we concentrate on how hungry and guilty we are. No matter which way it goes, God's word and promise are ignored and forgotten.

Worries, no matter how much reason there might be for them, always come from the old Adam. They are the only gifts he can give us, and he gives us as much as he can, trying to convince us that we should always look to ourselves and ourselves alone. Then worries become a circle, one worry feeding on another and another until the circle closes in with no apparent escape. Soon the promise is forgotten altogether.

Looking to the promise

How's this circle going to be broken? Well, one thing's sure from the beginning—it's not going to be broken as long as we keep looking to ourselves. If you've ever had a bad attack of worries, you know that. It doesn't do a bit of good to say "don't worry" or "there's nothing to be afraid of" at such a time. Hearing such words, you just worry about being worried or get scared of being scared.

No, it takes a different kind of looking entirely—a looking away from ourselves to the promise. That's what the Spirit gives us as he speaks the promise to us.

God doesn't just say, "Don't worry," and then go away, leaving us in our fears. He says, "I promise to be your God and give you everything good." And then he keeps his word, giving us not only daily bread but the other things we need to live from day to day. Much of the time, he gives even more than we need.

God doesn't just say, "Don't feel guilty," either. He says, "Here's what I've done about your guilt. I have heaped it all on Christ and he's carried it for you, drowning all your sins and guilt in my grace."

God goes even further. He not only speaks this word to you day after day to assure you that you are forgiven—he comes to assure you that you are forgiven—he comes to be with you and each of us in the sacrament of the Lord's Supper, reassuring us again with the bread and the wine that he is our God and forgives us all things.

When you look to this promise, then, realizing that all of God's gifts are for you, everything changes. You don't have to look to yourself for your daily bread and the other things you need to live each day. You don't have to pretend that you must earn everything, worrying night and day about how you can get and grab some more. You aren't likely to ignore the gifts either, taking them for granted.

Hearing this promise, you can receive all that God gives you for what they are: gifts. And you can count on your Father to give you all you need. Then, when you see your daily bread as a gift, you can share it with others, passing on the gifts God gives to other people who haven't received as much as you have.

The same thing happens with the word of forgiveness. When God says to you, "In my name all your sins are forgiven," you don't have to worry about what he thinks of you—he's told you himself that he's not going to hold anything against you. You don't have to prove yourself to him, trying to whip up enough sincerity or goose pimples to show you deserve it. "I don't care whether you deserve it or not," God says, "you're mine—insincerity, doubts, guilt, and all."

When God forgives you so freely, you can do the same with your neighbors. That's why Jesus put the fifth petition together the way he did—"forgive us our trespasses as we forgive those who trespass against us." He's not trying to make a deal with us— the God who promises doesn't make deals. He forgives us our failures to forgive, too. But as he forgives us, he intends that forgiveness to go through us to our neighbors. As that happens, it's a sure sign that the Spirit is at work, forgiving us as he promised.

Realizing that God gives us all that we need as gifts makes all the difference, then. As long as the old Adam in us gives us eyes only for ourselves, our worries become whirlpools pulling us in deeper and deeper until finally it seems we'll drown in anxiety and guilt. The old Adam is such a worrier because he knows that he's going to die.

But as the Spirit gives us ears and eyes for the promise, calling out the new you who looks to the promise, each day becomes a gift. We can then pray for our daily bread and ask God to forgive us our sins as we forgive others in the certainty that God will hear us and give us these gifts, as he has promised.

That's freedom—freedom from the old Adam's worry, guilt, and fear; freedom for the joyful service of God's people. There's no other freedom like it. God's promise makes every day new.

Chapter 21

Deliverance

THE SIXTH PETITION

And lead us not into temptation.

What does this mean?

God tempts no one to sin, but we ask in this prayer
that God would watch over us and keep us so that
the devil, the world, and our sinful self may not
deceive us and draw us into false belief, despair,
and other great and shameful sins. And we pray that
even though we are so tempted we may still win
the final victory.

THE SEVENTH PETITION

But deliver us from evil.

What does this mean?

We ask in this inclusive prayer that our heavenly
Father would save us from every evil to body and
soul, and at our last hour would mercifully take us
from the troubles of this world to himself in heaven.

The key to just about any good play in football, hockey, or basketball is the fake—making it seem as if you're going to do one thing when actually you're planning to do something else. When they work, fakes throw the defense off guard, opening up weaknesses that enable the offense to score or move closer to it.

There is nothing fake about temptations. They are terribly real. But they can be awfully deceptive, too. The less dangerous ones—temptations to curse, lust, steal or lie—can look the most powerful. And the most dangerous temptations—like false belief and despair—can look weak and harmless. While you're setting up a defense against the temptations you see most clearly, the more dangerous ones come along from the other direction, hitting you blindside to rob you of the freedom and hope of the promise.

Luther sometimes called the smaller temptations "fox tails" that tickle, or "puppy sins." It's not that they aren't difficult or harmful. It's just that they are weak in comparison to the big ones, which always come silently or secretly to attack God's word for us.

Jesus has given us the Sixth and Seventh Petitions for both kinds of temptation. But he is especially concerned with the big ones. So in the Sixth Petition, "lead us not into temptation," he teaches us to ask God for help with our temptations now, to keep us in faith while we await the new day. And in the Seventh, the concluding petition, he teaches us to pray also for the last day, when God will remove us from all temptations and every evil to take us to himself.

That leaves us with a couple of questions. First, what are these temptations that are so powerful? And second, how does God help us with them?

The hidden tempters

Something strange happens as God makes the new you. You might expect that this new you would get stronger and stronger until finally you wouldn't be tempted at all. That's partially true —the new you does get stronger in the promise.

But with temptation, it's just the opposite. The more you hear and want God's promise, the stronger the temptations get. It's like learning to drive—the more you learn, the more aware you become of the dangers.

The example Paul uses is coveting. "I should not have known what it is to covet if the law had not said, 'You shall not covet'" he says (Rom. 7:7). Maybe the same thing happened to you. Before you knew what coveting was, you probably didn't think there was anything wrong with dreaming about what belongs to your neighbors. More than likely you didn't consider it such a temptation, then, but something natural, something everyone does. But now that you know what's wrong with coveting, how the old Adam uses it to fill us with false hopes that put us at odds with our neighbors and finally to burn us out, maybe you can see why it's so dangerous.

If you can, you've probably learned something else, too—that coveting is an awfully difficult temptation to handle. For some reason, the minute we're told we can't have something, we want it. That's coveting. And the harder we try not to covet, the more covetous we become.

That's how the big temptations work—they are as sneaky and silent as coveting, and just as difficult. Their target is the promise of the First Commandment, God's promise—given to us in Christ —that he will be our God. Two of these big temptations are listed in Luther's explanation: false belief and despair.

To start with, false belief might not seem like much of a temptation—not nearly as tempting as gossiping or coveting. What does it matter what people believe, after all? Isn't it a free country?

That's the fake—false belief looks harmless at first. But now take a look at it. What is false belief? Since God's decision and promise to be our God in Christ, forgiving us and making us his own, is the most important belief we have, false belief would have to be something that denies that some way.

That's the heart of false beliefs. All of them say, in one way or another, that God's decision isn't enough or good enough for us. So, either they say that we ourselves have to do what God has promised to do, or they say that God goes partway and we go the rest of the way for him. The God of the promise is treated like a liar, then, and you lose the freedom and hope of the promise.

146

Do you find that tempting? Probably not, when it's put that way. But the old Adam is the master of disguise. He puts much nicer clothing on it to make it more attractive.

"It doesn't matter what you believe as long as you're sincere," the old Adam will say, as if God had never given us his word and we could make up anything we want about him. If that doesn't work, the old Adam will flip the coin so it comes down on the other side, making the promise into a law. "Now you have to believe this," he'll say, "and believe it just as I tell it to you—otherwise, there is no hope for you," as if God were some half-wit and his word so stupid that we have to be forced to accept it. Either way, the hope and joy of the promise is denied.

The second powerful temptation Luther lists in his explanation of the Sixth Petition is despair. Again, that doesn't sound like much of a temptation. But when things start to go wrong, when nothing seems to go the way you hope it will, it seems only natural to despair—to lose heart, to get down in the mouth or discouraged.

It's not surprising that things go bad sometimes, either, going from bad to worse. Even though God controls his opponents—the devil, the world, and our own flesh—they can still do enough damage to make us feel helpless and hopeless.

That's what makes despair such a sneaky temptation. It seems so natural. And that's what makes it so difficult to fight, too. Like

"We ask God to keep us from false belief and despair."

worries and guilt, despair and hopelessness feed on themselves, pulling us in deeper and deeper until finally there seems to be no way out. And then, fight though we may, God's word and promise don't seem true or helpful for us. The freedom and hope God promises to us in his word are lost for us, covered by the old Adam's despair.

So we pray, "lead us not into temptation," asking that God will watch over so that we don't get lured into such things as false belief and despair. Praying this petition, we are asking God to protect us now from anything that would lead us away from his promise, or put us at odds with our neighbors and the earth.

Power in weakness

The Apostle Paul tells a story in 2 Corinthians 12 that shows how God helps us in temptation. Paul says that he had a "thorn in the flesh," something that bothered him deeply. "Three times I besought the Lord about this," he says, "that it would leave me; but he said to me, 'My grace is sufficient for you, for my power is made perfect in weakness'" (vs. 8-9).

That's another puzzling answer, isn't it? He refused to take away whatever it was that bothered Paul. But still God gave Paul all that he could ask for and more: his grace.

That's how God helps us. Now, while we wait for the new day, God doesn't take us out of temptation, somehow making us immune to it or exempt from it. He's going to keep us here, where there is temptation, because this is where our jobs are.

But if God doesn't take us out of temptation, he gives us what he gave to Paul: grace that never ends, gifts on top of gifts, enabling us to live in temptation with faith and our hopes up. "My grace is sufficient for you," he says, "for *you*." It is the grace of his promise that he is your God, that he is making the new you who will be what he created you to be, a believer. It is the grace of his promise that he takes you as you are, putting the old Adam to death in you and promising to raise you from the dead. It is the grace that comes to you in his word and sacraments, assuring you and reassuring you that whatever happens, he is yours and you are his.

That's how Jesus fought the tempter—with God's word and promise of grace. When Jesus was led into the wilderness to be

148

tempted, he didn't rely on his own strength or power, as he very well could have. Instead, each time the devil came to him Jesus met him with the word. "It is written," Jesus said, "Man shall not live by bread alone but by every word that proceeds from the mouth of God'" (Matt. 4:4).

The word is the power God gives us in our weakness. We shall be tempted right up to our last day and hour. If it weren't for God's promise of grace, we would be beaten by temptations right up to the last hour, too. But God has filled our ears with his word and promise, encouraging us, comforting us, upholding and uplifting us. His word is his power, the power of his Spirit to uphold us in our weakness, to overcome all the temptations we face, to win the victory for us.

But that's not the end of the story. At our last hour, when the last day comes, God is going to deliver us from all evil—anything and everything that threatens us in any way. He is going to destroy all of his enemies—the old Adam, the rebellious world, and the devil—making us and his creation completely new.

Who is going to do that? Your heavenly Father—the one who in Christ taught you this prayer. He is the God of the promise, the God who raised Jesus from the dead, the God who will raise you from the dead. "Behold, I make all things new," he says (Rev. 21:5). "Amen," we say. That's the way it's going to be.

Chapter 22

How Do You Know?

"To obtain such faith God instituted the office of the ministry, that is, provided the Gospel and the sacraments. Through these, as through means, he gives the Holy Spirit, who works faith, when and where he pleases, in those who hear the Gospel."

Augsburg Confession   Article V

A big question has lurked behind the Commandments, the Creed, and the Lord's Prayer, ready to throw all they say into doubt. It has come up in our discussions a few times—maybe it has popped into your mind. The question is, "How do you know?"

Sometimes it can be the old Adam's question. When he asks, "How do you know?" it's generally with a blank look barely hiding a sneer. He's sure he has all the answers himself.

But this question can be asked in another way, too. It can come to each of us, not because we've made up our minds that there can't be an answer, but in the hope that somehow we can know, and know for certain, that God's decision and promise are meant for us.

What is the answer, then? How can we know that God's decision and promise are meant for each of us? Answer: Through the word and the sacraments God gives us in the church.

That answer may sound familiar, but you may be surprised. Together, the word and the sacraments are called the "means of grace." They are the vehicles God uses—the routes he takes—to give us his gifts and to show us that his promises are for us. Through them, "he gives the Holy Spirit, who works faith," as the Augsburg Confession says. In them, he calls out, sustains, fosters, nurtures, strengthens, upholds, and uplifts the new you in us to give us the certainty of his promise.

Hidden in the word

The first big surprise is in recognizing what common things God uses for the means of grace. You might expect God to overwhelm us—to come with crowds of angels or lightning flashes of glory. But look at what he uses: words, water, bread, and wine. You could hardly find four more ordinary things.

Words fill your day from morning to night; there is water just about everywhere; bread sits on practically every table; wine was the usual drink at meals in Bible times and, even if it's no longer customary for many people, it is still so common that it is available almost anywhere. Yet God takes these common and ordinary things and uses them to tell us he is our God and to make us his own.

This is the surprising thing about God's word, too. To speak to us, he makes his word just like one of ours—a word that rolls around the tongue and takes off between the teeth and lips to shake ear drums.

How has God done this? In Christ, first of all; then in the Bible, which bears witness to Christ; and finally in the spoken word, the word you hear as your pastor and others bear witness to Christ.

God's Word, first and foremost, is Christ. He not only spoke God's Word—he is God's Word, he did—he acted out—God's Word. "In the beginning was the Word," John says in his Gospel. "And the Word became flesh and dwelt among us, full of grace and truth; we have beheld his glory, glory as of the only Son from the Father" (1:1, 14).

In Christ, God became a person just like us, coming as close to us as our own flesh and blood. He was born just as we were;

ate, slept, and struggled as we do; and talked in a language like our own to tell us that he is our God and that we are his people. He said it in word and deed; he took upon himself our sin and our death; he was raised from the dead for us. Christ is God's Word—he said it and did it for us.

God's Word also comes to us through the Bible. It, too, is common and ordinary in many ways. It is printed on paper with ink and bound in covers like any other book. And it tells of ordinary people—men and women who believe and doubt, who wonder how they can know for sure, who struggle and fight.

But Christ sets the Bible apart from other books. He makes it holy; he makes the Bible God's Word. Because the Bible tells his story, from beginning to end, it is God's Word. Through it, God speaks to us, telling us all that he has said and done and will do in Christ.

The third way God speaks to us is another surprise, but one we've hinted at before. God speaks to us through preaching—the

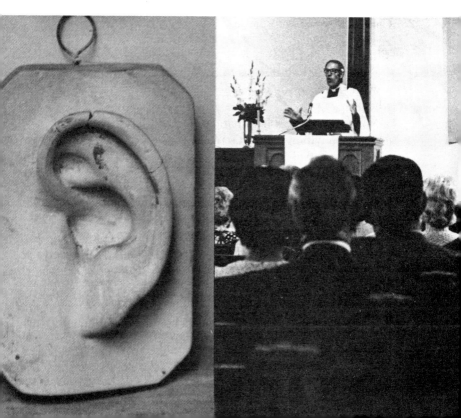

preaching and teaching of pastors and others as they bear witness to Christ.

God doesn't speak through your pastor's preaching and teaching because your pastor is holier than you, or because of any special quality pastors might possess. Rather, God speaks to you through your pastor's preaching and teaching as your pastor bears witness to Christ. As preachers proclaim the word to you, telling you of God's decision and promise to be your God, of Christ's death and resurrection, God is giving you his word.

God speaks to you through other people, too. As your parents, grandparents, brothers, sisters, cousins, friends or Sunday school teachers have told you of Christ, God has been speaking through them. You know for sure that they are ordinary people, but that's how God speaks—through words like our words spoken by people who talk like other people.

So this is God's Word, then, and this is how it comes to us. First, above all, and always, God's Word *is* Christ. The Bible is God's Word *because* it bears witness to Christ. And preaching and teaching are God's word *insofar as* they also bear witness to Christ, telling of his promise.

The living word

But that's not all there is to it. God's word is living and active, a word that snaps and crackles with life, making things happen wherever it goes.

Not every word is like that. Some words are just words. They don't do anything to you. When somebody tells you it is a quarter past two in Hong Kong or that winters can be cold, it doesn't make much difference to you.

But other words are alive. If someone you had been day-dreaming about suddenly came up to you and said, "I love you," the words could set you on fire. Or if the strongest person in your neighborhood stopped you and said, "I'm going to beat your brains in," the words would either bring up your fists or set your legs in motion. Words like those are powerful—they do things, making things happen in and to you.

This is how God's word works. Only it is much more powerful. When he said, "Let there be light," there was light. When

154

Jesus said, "Rise, take up your bed and go," a man who had been unable to move a muscle jumped to his feet (Mark 2:2-12).

Sometimes, though, God's word can seem so common and ordinary, so much like any other word, that it doesn't appear to do much. When you read the Bible, for instance, you might not always catch the promise in what is being said. Or when somebody starts explaining ideas about God, the ideas might sound okay, but may never make you want to live or die for them.

Jesus didn't write books or give lectures explaining theories about God. He told all kinds of stories and parables to make sure people understood the promise. But he always spoke the promise directly, person to person. "The kingdom of God is at hand," he said, "repent and believe in the gospel" (Mark 1:15). "Blessed are the poor in Spirit," he said, for theirs is the kingdom of heaven" (Matt. 5:3). "I am the resurrection and the life; he who believes in me, though he die, yet shall he live, and whoever lives and believes in me shall never die," he said (John 11:25-26).

That's how God's word is meant to come to you, also: as a promise, spoken to you by another person. God speaks commands to you, too, to keep the old Adam in line. But he has made his word a common, ordinary, human word so that it can be spoken, so that you can hear it, so that it can be shouted, sung, whispered by one person to another. That's the whole purpose of the church—to hear the word and speak it, to receive the sacraments and share them.

How can you know, then? How can you be sure? Listen! Open your ears! Somebody is going to say it to you: "God has promised to be your God—to give you everything good, to forgive your sin, to raise you from the dead!" When you hear that, the words are going to do something to you.

The words may make you fight. You may doubt them, struggle with them, or take God's promise as too common or ordinary. But someday God is going to use his word to make a believer out of you. Then you'll be sure, no matter how much you struggle. For it is God himself who speaks to you in his promise, God working through his Spirit to "work faith, when and where he pleases."

155

Unit 4

Chapter 23

The Greatest Miracle

What is Baptism?

Baptism is not water only but it is water used
together with God's Word and by his command.

What is this Word?

In Matthew 28 our Lord Jesus Christ says:
"Go therefore and make disciples of all nations
baptizing them in the name of the Father
and of the Son and of the Holy Ghost."

By the looks of it, you might never guess that Baptism is the
greatest miracle that happens to a person in a lifetime. It looks so
ordinary—some parents, some sponsors, and a pastor gathered
around a bowl to say a few words and splash some water on a
baby who either sleeps or screams, unaware of what's happening.
Who'd ever guess there is anything earthshaking or miraculous
about that?

But that's just like the God of the promise—to hide the most
miraculous event in a simple ceremony. Baptism is a miracle—
a miracle greater than walking on water or pulling handicapped
people out of wheelchairs. For in it, with the washing of water
and the pronouncement of his word, God himself declares each

156

of us to be his own, takes us into the communion of saints, and gives us a future that not even death and the devil can destroy.

But how do we know this? How do any of us know that God has done all this in our Baptism? That's the question we're going to consider in this chapter. For Baptism gives the certainty that God's decision is for us. This certainty comes through the combination of water with the word in God's command.

A watery beginning

In the last chapter we talked a little bit about the power in words. Some words are dead—they don't do anything to you or for you. But other words, like "I love you" or "I hate you," are alive—they make things happen, causing you to react in some way. Even simple words like "It's cold today" or "It's raining outside" have life in them—they make you put on gloves or wear a raincoat.

God's word is the original lively word. In fact, it is so powerful that God told Jeremiah his word is like a fire, "like a hammer that breaks the rocks to pieces" (23:29). And he said to Isaiah, "so shall my word be that goes forth from my mouth; it shall not return to me empty, but it shall accomplish that which I purpose, and prosper in the thing for which I sent it" (55:11). When God speaks his word it doesn't fail—it does what he says it will!

But when God's word is spoken to us by others in the church, other things can happen to it. The words we speak aren't always so lively. Even words like "I love you" can lose their power and joy.

So when we hear God's word spoken to us by someone else, it doesn't always seem to be a lively, life-giving word that opens up the future for us. And sometimes, when it is spoken to all kinds of people, it can leave us wondering if this word is really meant for us. For instance, when you hear Jesus' words from John 15:16, "You did not choose me, but I chose you," you might wonder if Jesus has really chosen you, too.

That's why Christ has given us the sacraments. He wants to make sure that his word and promise come home to us in a way we can't miss, as lively, life-giving words and promises that

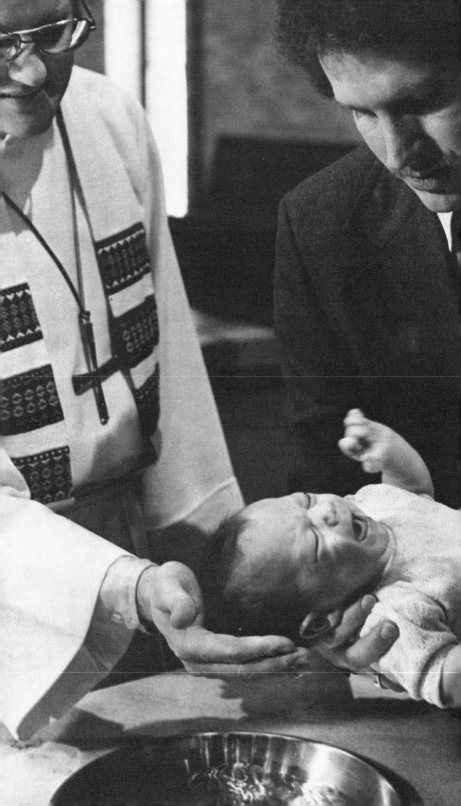

take hold of us, filling us with confidence in him. He wants to make sure there is no mistake about it—that each of us knows that his promises are meant precisely, exactly, and completely for us.

So in the sacraments Christ puts his words together with some common, ordinary earthly things—water, bread, and wine—to give his gifts to us. This combination—Christ's giving us his word with something earthly or physical—is what makes it a sacrament.

That's why Baptism is a watery beginning. In it, Christ takes plain ordinary water that has been drawn from a tap and puts it together with his word to seal you as his own. It is as if he says, "Here now, with the washing of this water, you know that my word and decision are for you. Now you can be certain, for I have washed you in my promise."

The word in the wash

The old Adam's favorite attack on Baptism is to ignore the word and concentrate on the water. "Water!" he sniffs. "Water! Whoever heard of such a thing? You flush your toilets with water and now you say that God uses water to make you certain? Nonsense!"

If that doesn't work, the old Adam puts on some religion and tries to explain Baptism away. "Oh yes," he'll say, "the water is a nice symbol. But what really counts is what you do with your Baptism. If you want to be sure of it, you have to make your Baptism complete by doing what God wants you to do."

Either way, whether by scorning the water or calling it a symbol, the old Adam makes it sound as if Baptism is "water only." Then it can be ignored as a quaint little ceremony for children, or taken as something we have to do before getting down to what's really important: doing good things for Jesus. It's the same story. If the old Adam doesn't ignore the promise completely, he insists on trying to earn what God will only give as a gift.

But "Baptism is not water only," as Luther's explanation says. "It is water used together with God's Word. . . ." The water and the Word can't be separated, not without losing the sacrament.

Apart from the Word, the water is plain, ordinary water. Apart from the water, the Word is still God's Word but the sacrament is gone. The Word and the water go together, the Word telling us what happens in the washing.

"Make disciples of all nations," Jesus said. How does this happen? By "baptizing them in the name of the Father, and of the Son, and of the Holy Spirit, and teaching them to observe all that I have commanded you." That is Christ's word, telling us what happens in the washing. As the word is spoken, as the water is washed across our heads, he makes us his disciples, his own beloved people.

So, in the speaking of his word and the washing of the water, he gives birth to the new you in each of us, making us members of his church. Then, after our Baptism, he continues to be with us in the teaching of his word and the Lord's Supper, sustaining and keeping the new you he has made. "And lo, I am with you always, to the close of the age," he says (Matthew 28:20).

That's why Baptism rings and sings with so much certainty. Where the old Adam can manage to separate the water from the word, the certainty is lost. But when the Word and the water work together, as Christ promises they do, Baptism is more certain than the sunrise. For Christ himself is present in the Word, with the water, to make us his very own and give us all the gifts he has to give.

The loving command

There is one more essential ingredient in Baptism—Christ's command. "Go therefore . . . ," he says, "make disciples . . . baptizing them. . ." That's an order.

Maybe it seems strange that Christ should command such a great and gracious gift. When Baptism is so full of his gifts, it's hard to understand why the whole world doesn't clamor for it, demanding to be baptized in his name.

But the truth is closer to the opposite. There is no gift, next to Christ himself, that the old Adam, the world, and the devil hold in deeper contempt. Baptism is the old Adam's funeral— the birth of the new you. So the old Adam attacks this sacrament with all the contempt, scorn, spite, malice, and hatred he can muster.

160

All of the old Adam's attacks on Baptism have the same purpose: to make it appear that it is something we do for God, not something God does for us. As a result, people wind up fearing, loving, and trusting in what they do, and Baptism finally doesn't matter. So pagans and unbelievers sneer at Baptism as a magic rite we do so we won't be afraid to die. Or the super-pious ignore Baptism as if God can't do what he promises, and concentrate on their own conversions, decisions for Christ, and "experiences" as far more important. Either way, Baptism is treated with complete contempt.

In all of these attacks, the fact that Christ commanded Baptism makes us all the more certain. It is a friendly command, a loving order Christ gives to us so that we will know how important Baptism is both to him and to us. Because he commanded it, we can be sure that Baptism is no human plaything—something invented by people to make us feel better. And we can be sure, too, that all of the old Adam's religious strutting about "conversions" and "experiences" is just that—strutting and nothing else.

Baptism is God's act for us. Though the pastor speaks the Word and does the washing, God is the one who baptizes. He is at work in every Baptism, putting his Word with the water to give us all his gifts. He keeps right on working, too, "to the end of the age" to be sure we're sure—to keep the new you in the certainty that is his gift.

Chapter 24

Off the Merry-go-round

What benefits does God give in Baptism?

In Baptism God forgives sin, delivers from death
and the devil, and gives everlasting salvation to
all who believe what he has promised.

What is God's promise?

In Mark 16 our Lord Jesus Christ says:
"He who believes and is baptized will be saved;
but he who does not believe will be condemned."

How can water do such great things?

It is not water that does these things, but God's
Word with the water and our trust in this Word.
Water by itself is only water, but with the Word of
God it is a life-giving water which by grace gives
the new birth through the Holy Spirit.
St. Paul writes in Titus 3:
"He saved us . . . in virtue of his own mercy,
by the washing of regeneration and renewal in the
Holy Spirit, which he poured out upon us richly
through Jesus Christ our Savior, so that we might
be justified by his grace and become heirs
in hope of eternal life. The saying is sure."

Your Baptism was the last judgment in miniature. As the word was spoken and the water washed across your head, God told you what his verdict on you is and what it will be when the last day comes. "Not guilty," he said. "This child is mine." Then, having rendered his verdict, God gave you all the gifts of the last judgment: forgiveness, deliverance, and everlasting salvation.

As the old Adam sees it, there has to be a catch somewhere. "How in the world can God do that?" he asks. "What's he trying to do? Bribe me? What does he want? We must have to do something!" So he hunts around, trying to find some kind of hidden agenda or concealed price tag to Baptism.

"Aha," the old Adam says, "here it is. We have to believe it—that's the price tag. If you don't believe, you'll never get these gifts. It says so right in the Catechism—'everlasting salvation to *all who believe* what he has promised,' '*he who believes* and is baptized,' 'God's word with the water *and our trust* in this word.' That's what you have to do," he says, "now get busy and believe it."

There's method to the old Adam's madness. If he succeeds in convincing you that this is a condition we must meet if we are to receive God's promise, he'll drive you into a circle that doesn't end. His chase will be on again.

God doesn't work that way, though. There is no catch, no trap, no hidden agenda or price tag to Baptism. It is a sheer gift, freely given. God wants you to believe that, and expects you

to. But he's not waiting for you to come up with enough belief or trust on your own. He gives what he commands, making a believer out of you by putting the old Adam to death and raising up the new you with his gifts.

We'll look at the old Adam's endless circle first, and then consider how God gives us the faith to go with his promises.

The circle

Do you ever wonder what kind of impression you make on people? That seems to concern all of us at one time or another. And it can be painful, too, especially in regard to people who are important, whose impression of us matters.

The pain is in the wondering and doubting, as you try to figure out what people you admire really think of you. You might see some signs that they do respect you, that they're willing to be considered your friends. But then you might see some signs on the other side, too. They might not take time to talk with you, for instance, or you might not be invited along with them to something special. When that happens you can begin to feel rejected, left out, unliked or unlikable.

What happens then? Well, you might decide that those people really weren't worth that much concern anyway, that you're better off without them. Or you might decide that you have to try harder, doing some things to make sure you make the kind of impression you want.

It might work to try harder. But it can turn out another way, too. If you try to make impressions, you can get caught on a merry-go-round where every effort to impress just makes you wonder and doubt all the more. You might buy some new clothes, for instance, and still wonder if they produce the right effect. You might try again by telling stories about your accomplishments. If that didn't work, you might try something different. Pretty soon you would be going in circles—trying, wondering, trying, wondering, never quite sure what the people you wanted to impress really thought of you.

When the old Adam succeeds in tying a condition to Baptism, making it appear that we have to show God how much we believe before he'll give us his gifts, the same merry-go-round

164

starts. We try to believe and then wonder if we've believed enough, try again and wonder some more, constantly working to come up with something that will put our doubts to rest.

It's like a story a Swedish lady told about a pastor in her country. The man was glad he was humble, she said, because he knew that Christians should be humble. But then he was sad

that he was glad that he was humble, because a person who is really humble shouldn't be glad about it. But then he was glad that he was sad that he was glad that he was humble, because at least when he was sad about being glad, he was humble again.

That's just how it works. When we start trying to manufacture our own faith, trying to drum up enough trust to show God that we really deserve the promise, the merry-go-round keeps turning. We start putting faith in our faith, trusting our own trust, believing that we deserve the promise because we believe. That's not faith or trust in God and his promises, but faith in ourselves and what we've done or are doing. It's just one more of the old Adam's tricks.

The faith God gives

God doesn't send us on this kind of wild goose chase. He doesn't expect us to believe by our own effort or strength. Rather, he gives us faith as his gift. He himself provides the belief and trust in us that go with his promises. How? In the Word, in Baptism and the Lord's Supper!

Look again at that concern for making good impressions. Some people make you feel that you have to do something special to impress them. But there are other people, even if they're rare, who let you know in small ways or large that they are already impressed with you, that they care for you and will accept you even when your sore spots show.

Good friends are like that. You don't have to impress them. They're already impressed enough with you to like and respect you, even when you're at your worst. You can relax with them and be yourself without worrying what they think of you.

How do you learn to trust friends like that so completely? It's not by command. If somebody you didn't know came up to you and said, "Now you have to be my friend and trust me completely," you'd either ask why, excuse yourself politely, or turn around and run. No, you learn to trust close friends because they show you, in small ways and large, that they can be trusted.

That's how God gives us the faith that goes with his promises. In Baptism he says, "Christ has given me my impression of you.

166

In Christ, I have the best impression possible—the impression that you're not guilty, that you're one of mine and worth keeping forever. But that's not just my impression—it's my decision, word, and promise to you." Having said it, God acts on it, giving you his gifts.

And that's just the beginning. From Baptism onward, God sends his Spirit to work in us day after day to make believers out of us. He speaks to us in the word, assuring us that God holds nothing against us and will not allow anything to separate us from him. He gives us the word again and again to reassure us that having decided to be our God, he is going to raise us from the dead. And he comes to be with us in the Lord's Supper to renew us in his gifts, to put us on the way again. All the while, the Spirit surrounds us with others in the church. He is always at work to give us faith, to hold us and keep us in it. He is full of gifts, and always giving.

That's just what the old Adam can't believe. "It can't be a gift," he says, "somehow there has to be a catch to it. The world doesn't work that way—there's a catch to everything, you get what you pay for, you have to win friends and influence people. Think what would happen if God just gave these gifts. How

would anyone ever be good if it weren't for a reward? And what about people who are baptized and never do anything about it? What about people who aren't baptized at all? There must be something we have to do ourselves to get what we want from God."

"No," God says, "there isn't a catch. All I have to give is yours, and I've given it to you in your Baptism, as a gift. All I want is to make a believer out of you. And I'm doing that myself. I'm making you what I want you to be. I started in your Baptism, and I'm going to keep at it until the day I take you to myself."

Seeing that, recognizing and receiving the gift, is what finally destroys the old Adam. God's gifts are the death of him. For when you recognize the gift, you can see that all of the old Adam's attempts to impress God are worthless, just so much religious junk the old Adam puts on display to show himself off. It is manufactured faith, sham religion, that is designed to impress God and others without asking too much of you. Finally, it can only drive you into the circle, putting you on the merry-go-round again.

But at the same time, when you recognize the gift, you can see how the new you is born in the water and the word of Baptism. It is the you God is setting free. Knowing the promise of Baptism, you are free from having to impress God. You are free to call upon him, asking him to give you the belief and trust he promises to give. You are free from having to impress your neighbors with the old Adam's religion. You are free to speak the word to your neighbors, telling them of all God does and gives. You are free from having to wonder and doubt what the future and God's judgment will be. You are free to believe what he has already told you, tells you, and will keep telling you in the church: "He who believes and is baptized shall be saved." That's you. You can be sure of it.

Chapter 25

Letting Go to Take Hold

What does Baptism mean for daily living?

It means that our sinful self, with all its evil
deeds and desires, should be drowned through
daily repentance; and that day after day a new
self should arise to live with God
in righteousness and purity forever.
St. Paul writes in Romans 6:
"We were buried therefore with him by Baptism
into death, so that as Christ was raised from
the dead by the glory of the Father,
we too might walk in newness of life."

Jesus once pictured repentance with a surprising little parable. "The kingdom of God is like a treasure hidden in a field," he said, "which a man found and covered up; then in his joy he goes and sells all that he has and buys that field" (Matt. 13:44).

If you've thought of repentance as a tearstained remorse complete with a sincere desire to do better, this parable might not sound much like it. Apparently the man wasn't even looking for a treasure—he just stumbled across it. And then, instead of advertising in the lost and found or telling the owner, he rushed out to scrape up enough money to buy the field. It makes you wonder if he was completely honest.

But both parts of the movement Jesus called repentance are in this little story. First, because the treasure was so great, the man sacrificed everything he had to get it. Then, he ran to buy the field, to take hold of the treasure.

Luther emphasizes both parts of the movement in his explanation of what Baptism means for daily living. As God gives his gifts, the old Adam dies each day and a new self, the new you, arises, getting wrapped up in the promise. We'll look at how this happens.

The drowning

With vaults and Swiss bank accounts available, the days when robbers—or crooked politicians—left buried treasures behind them are long gone.

But you may have found a treasure in another way, and gone through the same kind of a movement the man in the parable

did. Maybe, for instance, you've discovered that you are a much better student or athlete than you once thought. Or maybe you've found that you have some special talent—for music, mechanics, or a game—which you didn't realize you had but which has now become very important to you.

If something like that has happened, you've experienced the first side of this movement. For instance, suppose you were told one day that you have a fine ear and would make a very good musician. A talent like that could open all kinds of doors for you. It could give you joy and a purpose, bringing you other people's respect and appreciation.

Then, just for the joy of being good at your music, you would let go of some other things that had been important to you before. You might quit watching a lot of television, for instance, or lose some early morning sleep so that you could practice. You might lose interest in some friends who were once important to you, and gain some new friends who shared your interest. You might even start skimming over other classes and homework to make more time for practicing and listening to music.

Sometimes these sacrifices would be easy. You'd make them without thinking, without ever realizing they were sacrifices. Other times, the sacrifices might be difficult. But as long as the joy of music was close, you'd keep on letting go of other things, clearing them away, to get at it.

If you've gone out for a sport, played in a band, enjoyed a special class, tried to be a good student, or wanted to excel at something else, you know how it works. You keep clearing away what is less important to get at what's most important to you.

That's what the first side of the movement called repentance is like. When Jesus started preaching, he called for repentance in no uncertain terms. But he didn't just say "repent!" and then turn away, trying to make us feel rotten about ourselves so that we'd shed a few crocodile tears and whip up a sincere desire to do better. That would be the old Adam's merry-go-round again. Soon we'd be proud of being ashamed of ourselves—that wouldn't be repentance at all.

No, Jesus announced the gift and stayed with it. "The kingdom of God is at hand;" he said, "repent and believe in the gospel"

(Mark 1:15). First he proclaimed the gift, the surprising good news that God is coming to make us and the whole creation new. Then he talked about repentance, calling people to let go of everything else they'd clung to.

Jesus did the same with tax collectors and prostitutes. He didn't say, "When you've repented, I'll sit down at your table with you." He sat down with them, speaking the word to them, making his presence felt. And then, like Zaccheus, for the joy of the gift they repented (Luke 19:1-10).

He does the same with us in our Baptism. Most of us were baptized as infants, before we even knew there was such a thing. That's how God works: he comes straight out with it, promising to give us all the gifts he has to give, to forgive us, destroy the grave for us, and make us and the whole creation new.

Then comes the repentance, not because we must impress Jesus with how penitent we are, but just because his gifts are so great. Like the hidden treasure, the gifts are buried in a simple ceremony of water and words. But as we receive them, we find out how great and precious these gifts are. And then the wheels of repentance are set in motion. Then, like the man who found a treasure hidden in a field, or like you when you've suddenly discovered you're really good at something, we say, "Sell the rest —let everything else take second place. I want this."

There's some sorrow in it, too—the sorrow of recognizing how in our attempts to impress God we treat him as a liar; the sorrow of realizing how we've harmed our neighbors and ourselves. And there's the sorrow of making some difficult sacrifices, letting go of some things that have been important. But it's not the pat-me-on-the-back-because-I've-been-so-sincerely-sorry kind of sorrow. It's the sorrow in the midst of joy that comes when we let go of some things that used to be important—because now what's really important has come.

That's how the old Adam dies. God kills the old you each day with kindness. He keeps showering you with his promises and gifts until finally the old you just plain dies of it. It happens as the Spirit working through the word enables you to say, "I don't have to impress God anymore, or prove that I can take care of myself. I can count on him to keep his word. I repent—you are the Lord. Do what you think is best."

The rising

That's the first side of the movement called repentance—the letting go. Once that's started, the other side follows—taking hold of the gift. "Sell everything," the man in the parable said, "so I can buy that field." "Let everything else go," someone who wants to be good at something says, "I want to do this"— to be a good musician, a good student, a good mechanic or something else.

As this happens, as the gift takes hold of you, your whole way of looking at things changes. Again, take music for an example. If you didn't think you had a talent for it or didn't enjoy it, you might think that music teachers are fussy and unreasonable, that music students are strange, that the music taught in school or by piano teachers is pretty dull.

"As the gift takes hold of you, your whole way of looking at things changes."

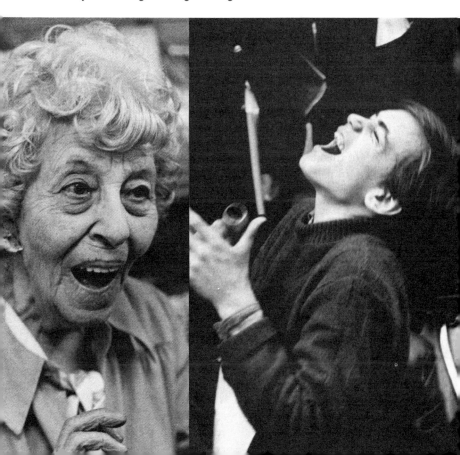

But if you found out that you really had a talent for it, all of that would change. Then you'd be all ears for your music teacher, taking in every word in hopes of improving. The other music students would become your companions, people you help and who help you. And music itself, all kinds of music, would take on new excitement.

Everything turns around

That's what happens on the second side of repentance, too. Once God's gifts and promises take hold of you, your whole way of looking at things turns around, so that as Paul says, you "walk in newness of life."

Then God is no longer a glorified fire extinguisher that hangs on the wall for emergencies only. He is your God, your heavenly Father, the one to whom you turn at all times. Then instead of wondering why your neighbors are so strange, trying to impress them or go them one better, you begin to see the people in your church and other people as friends—people who hear the word with you, people to be loved and cared for, people who love and care for you.

And then, instead of seeing your life as just one day after another when you have to try to grab the future, you can begin to see your life in terms of God's purposes for you—to serve him, to love your neighbors, to care for the earth. That's the new self that arises, the new you born in the water and word of Baptism.

All of this doesn't happen automatically, though. For one thing, the sinful self, the old Adam, doesn't just drop dead and never return. Though Baptism is his death, he doesn't finally die until you do. And in the meantime, he rages, struggles, fights, quivers, shakes, and rattles as viciously and dangerously as a dying lion, trying to recover.

For another thing, this world isn't the kingdom yet. The new creation has begun in Christ, but he has not yet destroyed all his enemies. As long as death remains, as long as the world wants to go its own way, you are going to have plenty of problems and struggles. And then there's the devil, God's mimic, always ready to fan your questions and doubts into a flame with more doubts and false promises.

174

That's why Baptism means a *daily* dying and rising, a daily drowning of the old Adam and a daily rising of the new you in you. Repenting and believing aren't habits—things that we acquire or have installed in us like the automatic pilots on planes. We don't just automatically forget about the other things that have been important to us. And we don't just automatically believe, either.

Then how does it happen? It happens day by day, as God sends his Spirit to speak to us through the word and to renew us in the sacraments.

"Remember your Baptism," the Spirit says. "As the old Adam fights and struggles, remember what God did when you were baptized—how he promised to make you, a crying baby, one of his own, to make you new and to bring you into his new creation to dwell with him."

"This is my word," the Spirit says as your pastors and others bear witness to Christ for you, "you are mine and all the gifts are yours." "This is the Lord's Supper," the Spirit says, "in it Christ is with you to open up the future to you."

In these ways, through the word and the sacraments he gives in the church, the Spirit will give you faith day by day and keep you in it. He'll set the wheels of repentance in motion in you, prying you away from whatever tries to take his place, wrapping you up in the promise. God sent his Spirit to you in your Baptism to do just that—to kill the old Adam in you, to raise up the new you day by day, to keep you and make you what you will be. You can be sure of it. God keeps his promises. It's for certain.

Unit 4

Chapter 26

More than a Memory

What is Holy Communion?

Holy Communion is the body and blood of our Lord
Jesus Christ given with bread and wine, instituted
by Christ himself for us to eat and drink.

Where do the Scriptures say this?

Matthew, Mark, Luke, and Paul say:
Our Lord Jesus Christ, in the night in which he was
betrayed, took bread; and when he had given thanks,
he broke it and gave it to his disciples, saying,
"Take, eat, this is my body, which is given for you;
this do in remembrance of me." After the same
manner also he took the cup after supper, and when
he had given thanks he gave it to them, saying,
"Drink of it, all of you; this cup is the new
testament in my blood, which is shed for you,
and for many, for the remission of sins; this do,
as often as you drink it, in remembrance of me."

Waiting can be both delicious and a torture. It's delicious
when it's waiting for something you want. Then, whether it's as
great as summer or as routine as supper, you've got something
to look forward to.

But it can be torturous, too. Somehow the clock always seems
to slow down during waiting times. And while you wait, there

can be all kinds of questions and worries about whether what you're waiting for is ever going to come.

That's the kind of situation we're in now as God's people. He's made his decision about us, and through Baptism and the word he's given us his gifts. But the new day hasn't come yet. We are waiting, between the times—the time of his promise and the time of his new day. We have the delicious hope of what is to come. But it is still a hope, and the waiting can be tortured by all kinds of questions and fears.

Christ doesn't leave us to stand and wait alone, though. While he gives us his gifts, he keeps us surrounded with other believers to wait and hope with us. But he goes further, much further. Besides giving us all the gifts of Baptism and speaking to us in the word, he gives us the Sacrament of the Altar: the Lord's Supper. In it, he himself comes to be with us in our between times to renew us in his gifts, to unite us as his people in the church, and to give us a taste of what the new day is going to be.

That's what is most important about this sacrament—Christ's presence with us as we eat and drink the bread and wine with one another.

Eating and drinking

The Lord's Supper goes by many different names, each one emphasizing some part of it. It is called Holy Communion because in it we have union with Christ and other Christians as we eat and drink. Christ participates with us and we who are baptized children participate with him and one another in his gifts (1 Cor. 10:16). It is also called the Sacrament of the Altar, because we gather around the altar to receive it; and the Eucharist, from a Greek word meaning "thanksgiving," because of the thanks and joy that go with Christ's gifts.

The best name for this sacrament, though, is the one used in the New Testament: the Lord's Supper (1 Cor. 11:20). It sums up in two words the most important ingredients of the sacrament.

First of all, it is the *Lord's* Supper. Christ instituted the sacrament at the last supper he ate with his disciples, commanding them—and us—to eat the bread and drink the wine in remembrance of him. Christ has the action in the sacrament. It is his

177

presence with us as we eat and drink, his giving himself to us with the bread and the wine, that renews us in his gifts and gives us a foretaste of what is to come.

Second, it is the Lord's *Supper.* As Christ gave bread and wine to his disciples to eat and drink, he gives bread and wine to us with his promise. Though the servings may be small, it is a meal, a supper. Just as Baptism is a washing in the word, the Lord's Supper is eating and drinking in the word. But while baptism happens to only one person at a time, in the Lord's Supper the whole congregation eats and drinks together.

So, again, the two main things that happen in the sacrament are Christ's giving of his promise and the eating and drinking.

But now we run into the same problem we met with the Sacrament of Holy Baptism. When you look at the Lord's Supper, it can look like a dressed up meal. The pastor speaks some words and the people do some eating and drinking. But the words are like our words—words that anyone can speak and understand. And the bread and wine are plain, ordinary bread and wine— the kinds that can be bought in a store.

Christ's presence with us

The difference between this meal and every other meal is that it is the *Lord's* Supper. He takes bread and says, "This is *my* body." He takes wine and says, "This cup is the new testament in *my* blood." It is this action, his presence with us, that makes the difference.

There are different ways of trying to understand how Christ is present with us in his supper. Some Christians have argued that Christ is only present in our memories; that since he has now ascended to God's right hand, he can't really be with us in the eating and drinking. As they see it, the sacrament is only a dramatic way of remembering what Christ once did for us.

Other Christians have argued that Christ becomes present with us in his supper by changing the bread and wine into his actual body and blood. This understanding is called "transubstantiation," or "changing substance." While the bread and wine still look like bread and wine, to this way of thinking their substance changes to become the body and blood.

The differences between these two understandings and the Lutheran understanding of the Lord's Supper are hidden in three small words in Luther's explanation: "Holy Communion *is* the body and blood of our Lord Jesus Christ *given with* bread and wine. . . ."

"Holy Communion *is* the body and blood of our Lord Jesus Christ. . . ." That little *is* says that Christ is more than a memory— that he is actually present with us as we eat and drink the bread and wine together. That is the heart of the gospel. When he first gave this supper to his disciples, Jesus didn't say about the bread, "this represents my body," or "here is a good way to remember my body." He said, "This *is* my body, given for you."

That makes all the difference. It means that the Lord's Supper isn't something we do for Jesus, getting together to have a meal in his memory. Rather, it is something Jesus does for us. He is risen from the dead, he is reigning right now as Lord of the future. He's not tied to some faraway place in the heavens. He can go where he wants and do what he wants. And he wants to be with us.

But now those other little words come along. "Holy Communion is the body and blood of our Lord Jesus Christ *given with* the bread and wine. . . ." The bread and wine don't change, in substance or in any other way, not any more than the water of Baptism changes. They remain common, ordinary bread and wine. But Christ's body and blood are *given with* them, or, as Luther also said, "in, with, and under the bread and wine."

Do you suppose that our God, who is always giving, would leave us stuck in the middle of our waiting time? The old Adam would like to think so. He'd like to make it seem that God is so far away that he never has the time or the interest to bother with the likes of us. And the old Adam would also like to make it seem that water, bread, and wine are too weak, common, and ordinary for God's uses.

But that's not the way God works. He is always with us; he never leaves us alone. He is always giving; he doesn't hold back.

Why this sacrament, then? If God is always with us, if he is always giving, why should he bother to give us the Sacrament of the Lord's Supper?

God gives it for you, for each of us, for our between times. As long as we're waiting, we're in jeopardy. And as long as we're in jeopardy, God wants to give himself to us in a way we can't miss. He wants to be sure that we're sure, to be certain we can be certain he's with us. So, in the Lord's Supper, Christ *gives* us his body and blood *with* the bread and wine. He takes common, ordinary earthly things and uses them to give himself completely. "Here I am," he says, "given for you."

In this way, Christ picks up and makes us new again. He reassures us that his word of forgiveness is meant precisely for each of us, putting his promise between our teeth so that we can chew it, pouring it out on our lips so that we can taste it, roll it around in our mouths, and swallow it. "This is my body, given for you," he says. "Now you have me. I am yours and you are mine."

In this way, Christ unites us as his people, too. His promise is given with the bread and wine to each of us as the Spirit gathers us together in the communion of the church. In Christ, your friends and neighbors who eat and drink the Lord's Supper with you become your brothers and sisters.

And in this way, Christ gives us a taste of what the end is going to be. "This is what it's going to be like," he says.

That's what makes the Lord's Supper such a great and precious gift. It's not some pious invention designed to give us a dramatic way of remembering Jesus. It is his supper, his gift to us. It is "instituted by Christ himself for us to eat and drink."

"Do this," he said, "Do this in remembrance of me." With this command, he lets us know that he wants to be with us while we wait. He is more than a memory—he is our Lord. With his command, we can be certain—certain that he's with us from beginning to end, now and always.

Unit 4

Chapter 27

Opening the Future

What benefits do we receive from this sacrament?

The benefits of this sacrament are pointed out by the words, *given and shed for you for the remission of sin.* These words assure us that in the sacrament we receive forgiveness of sins, life, and salvation. For where there is forgiveness of sins, there is also life and salvation.

How can eating and drinking do all this?

It is not eating and drinking that does this, but the words, *given and shed for you for the remission of sins.* These words, along with eating and drinking, are the main thing in the sacrament. And whoever believes these words has exactly what they say, forgiveness of sins.

When Christ forgives, he swings his gift like a double-edged axe. With one edge, he swings back to clear away all the brush and barriers that can tangle and block up our between times. With the other, he swings forward to clear the way to the future.

The promise of forgiveness may not seem that powerful. Sometimes it can seem more like a little hatchet, maybe even a rubber one, given to the guilt-ridden and the really religious to make them feel better about themselves.

But forgiveness packs all the power of God's promise. It is his barrier-breaking, future-opening gift. "For where there is forgiveness of sins," as Luther's explanation says, "there is also life and salvation." Forgiveness works that way in your daily life with your family and neighbors, opening things up for you. When God gives it, forgiveness does even more, opening up all his gifts.

Clearing the way

If you've ever been part of a family quarrel or had a skirmish with someone at school, you already have some idea of what forgiveness—or the lack of it—can do.

No matter how small or simple, quarrels set up barriers between people. Take a fight between friends, for instance. As long as friends get along, they can enjoy each other and be themselves when they are together without worrying. But when a quarrel gets started, all of that changes. The good times are replaced by hurt feelings, suspicion, dislike, and maybe some fear. The friendship gets blocked off.

These barriers close off the future, too. As long as friends enjoy each other, they look forward to chances to do things together—going to the movies on the weekend, for instance, or doing something special together during the summer. But when a quarrel breaks out, the future they looked forward to together is lost. They start avoiding one another.

A quarrel like this can become another one of the old Adam's merry-go-rounds. When one friend, accidentally or intentionally, hurts another, the friend who gets hurt will often repay the hurt in kind. Soon there can be revenge for the revenge and then maybe revenge for revenge for revenge, a full circle.

This doesn't only happen in quarrels, though. All kinds of things can make barriers between people. Even if it is as small as not liking the way someone looks, the dislike blocks a friendship. People who dislike you try to have as little to do with you as possible. Then you don't have any future with them. If you return the dislike, the circle is completed.

183

One way to stop merry-go-rounds like these is to declare a cease-fire. Quarreling friends, for instance, will sometimes just give up on each other. They stop fighting, but they don't heal the wounds. Leaving the barriers in place, they go their separate ways, former friends who don't fight anymore but don't have anything to do with each other either.

The only other way to break the circle is through forgiveness. It doesn't just stop it—it breaks it up entirely, clearing away the barriers and opening up the future again.

It's usually not easy. When you ask someone to forgive you, you admit a fault on your part. You're admitting, too, that you really want and need that person for a friend. It can be just as hard when someone asks you for forgiveness. If you do forgive such a person, you're admitting that you want and need the friendship, too.

But when forgiveness happens, everything opens up again. It is a new beginning. All that has stood between you and the other person is cleared away, and you have a future with that person again.

The same thing happens when people accept you the way you are, overlooking things that might make you unattractive.

When you are accepted, the barriers are broken and the future is opened—you can make friends and look forward to good times with people who take you the way you are.

That's how forgiveness works: it breaks down barriers and opens up the future.

One of the barriers that can come between God and us is our own guilt. It starts, like a quarrel, with something we do or fail to do—something we do that is obviously wrong or something we fail to do that clearly should have been done.

The old Adam knows what to do with guilt. Seizing it, he goes straight to work telling us that God cannot or will not have anything to do with the likes of us. Soon he has us going in circles, trying to prove to God that we're not so bad after all, or else convinced that God won't be our God any longer. Either way, guilt makes our future with God seem closed.

As painful as it can be, though, guilt isn't the only barrier. In fact, it's not even the biggest one. The big one, the tough one, is in what we are. It's the old Adam in us, the old worrier in you.

When the old you is worried, as it always is in one way or another, God seems far away. Then you either get so caught up in all you have to do each day that God doesn't seem to matter, or

else you become convinced that God is some kind of trader in the sky waiting for you to show how good you are before he'll take care of you.

Both of these are barriers—brush and blockades that come between God and you.

But "where there is forgiveness of sins, there is also life and salvation." When God speaks his word of forgiveness to you, when Christ gives you the gift of forgiveness in his supper, he takes the axe to those barriers and shatters and splinters them into a million pieces.

"This is my body," he says, "given for you." "This cup is the new testament in my blood, which is shed for you and for many for the remission of sins." It is as if Christ says, "Here I am, right here, with you. All of your guilt is destroyed. Everything that you've done and failed to do is wiped out."

The old Adam dies on these words. When he tries to insist that "God is so big and faraway he couldn't possibly be interested in all that you have to worry about," Christ says, "This is my body, given for you—I am with you and for you." When the old Adam says, "I have to prove to God that I am religious and deserving, that I'm not so bad after all," Christ replies, "This is my blood, shed for you. You don't have to prove anything. I'm giving myself to you completely."

With the barriers destroyed, the future opens up to you. Forgiveness isn't just a word for the past; it is a word for the future, too. When Christ says, "This is my body and blood given and shed for you," he is giving himself to us so that we can count on him for the future. Receiving his gifts, we can expect him to care for us and open the way to the new day he has promised.

His blood is "shed for you and for many," for you and for all who commune with you, whether in your congregation or in others throughout the world. In his Supper, Christ unites you with all of his people in the church so that you can look forward to the future in the company of his saints, caring for them and being cared for by them while you await the new day.

Receiving the gift

But there's one more question: how can eating and drinking bread and wine knock down barriers and open up the future?

If you remember the explanation of Baptism, you already know the answer. The Lord's Supper isn't eating and drinking alone any more than Baptism is water alone. It is eating and drinking in the word, and it's through the word that all the gifts come.

"Given and shed for you," Christ says, "*for you.*" Hearing these words as you eat the bread and drink the wine, you can be certain that all of Christ's gifts are meant for you.

That's how Christ, in the Spirit, renews the new you, giving you faith. When you hear the words "forgiveness of sins," you can be sure that Christ is at work clearing away every obstacle to open up the future. And when you hear the words, "Given and shed *for you* for the remission of sins," you can be certain that Christ is right there with you, "for you," to do just that. The certainty he gives is faith, "the assurance of things hoped for," as Hebrews calls it (11:1), the confidence that Christ's gifts and promises are meant for you.

Christ has seen to it that forgiveness is proclaimed and given to you over and over again. In this way, he brings us back to our Baptism, renewing us again and starting us afresh. And as he forgives he opens the way to the new day so that we can look forward to tomorrow and the next day with certainty and hope. That's what forgiveness does—it is Christ's barrier-breaking, future-opening gift.

"Forgiveness renews us and opens the future."

Chapter 28

Two Traps

*When is a person rightly prepared
to receive this sacrament?*

Fasting and other outward preparations serve a good
purpose. However, that person is well prepared and
worthy who believes these words, *given and shed for
you for the remission of sins.* But anyone who does
not believe these words, or doubts them, is neither
prepared or worthy, for the words *for you*
require simply a believing heart.

There are a couple of traps around the Lord's Supper that
are as old as the hills. But their teeth are still razor sharp, and
when they spring, they rip the joy out of our between times.

The first trap is the idea that we have to do something in order
to make the sacrament work. The second is the idea that the
sacrament works no matter what we do. In the first, Christ's
promise is made into a law; in the second, it's taken for magic.

Do you recognize the traps? They're just two different versions
of the same trick which the old Adam always uses to undermine
God's promise. We've seen them in every section of the Catechism.

There are good reasons for taking a hard look at these traps
again, though. For one thing, when the old Adam springs them
all the comfort and joy of the Lord's Supper is destroyed. For

another, the old Adam is going to keep setting and resetting them, varying and trying to spring them again, as long as you live.

We'll look at how these traps work and what they do, first of all. Then we'll see how we can expect Christ to keep his promise in his Supper, coming to be with us to uphold and renew us in our between times.

Who's in charge here?

The key to recognizing both of these traps is to notice the way the old Adam tries to take charge of the sacrament. That's one of the old Adam's trademarks—wanting to be in control, making what we do so important that what God is doing doesn't really matter.

Though they may look different, that's the purpose of both of these traps. They reverse things so that the old Adam, the old you in us, has the action while God sits by doing very little or nothing at all. The question to ask, then, is "Who's in charge here?" "Whose supper is it?"

The first trap, the idea that we have to do something to make the sacrament work, is the religious one. It has dozens of variations.

Sometimes the old Adam will come on full of sham holiness, talking about what a great gift the Lord's Supper is. "What bothers me, though," he'll say, "is how many people take it so lightly and insincerely." Other times, the old Adam will reverse his approach and talk about how religious and wonderful people can be without bothering with silly things like bread and wine. Or sometimes the old Adam will attack the pastor and those who administer the sacrament, saying that they're so irreligious and sinful that God could never give gifts where they're involved.

It's at this point—after making some complaint about the others who receive the Supper, the way it's given, or who gives it—that the old Adam hangs his price tag. "If you're going to get what God has to give," he says, "you have to do something about it. You have to prove to him that you're sincere, that you're trying hard, that you really don't want to do wrong anymore."

Now the fact that the old Adam is playing judge on other people who give or receive the Lord's Supper is a sure sign that he's up to no good. Holding court on the neighbors, without being elected or called to do so, is one of the old Adam's favorite games.

But that's not the real problem. When the old Adam gets by with this ploy, everything gets turned upside down so that what we do with the Lord's Supper matters as much as or more than what Christ does.

Though the old Adam would never come right out and say so, what the complaints and price tags really mean is this: "Christ doesn't know how to give his gifts. I have to help him somehow."

"The old Adam will come on full of sham holiness."

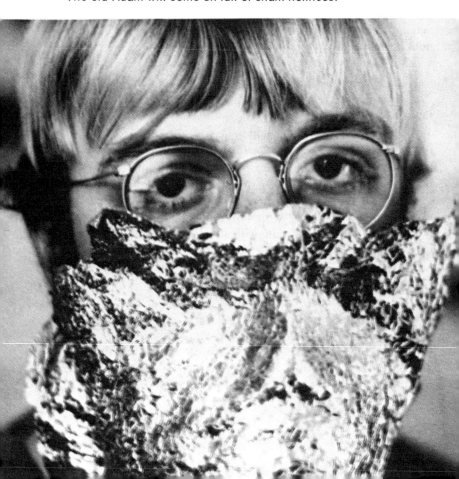

Or "Christ doesn't really know who he's giving these gifts to—these other people aren't nearly as worthy as I am." Or "Christ doesn't know who is helping him give these gifts—I am so much better than they are."

Do you see what this does to the Lord's Supper? It treats Christ as a liar, taking him for someone so poor and incompetent that he doesn't know what he's doing. It makes Communion into a law—something we have to do in order to impress Jesus or somehow win his favor.

And it puts us right back onto the old Adam's merry-go-round again. Pretty soon we're so worried about how we look, act, and feel when we go to the Supper that there's no comfort or joy in it at all. It's no wonder people go to the Lord's Table looking as though they face some kind of painful innoculation. The trap has sprung.

The second trap

The other trap isn't as pious looking. But it's really the other side of the same coin. In this one, the old Adam says that the sacrament works no matter what we do.

Now again, this trap has all kinds of variations. Sometimes the old Adam will try to spring it very religiously. He'll start out with all kinds of praise for the sacrament, talking about how wonderful it is that God takes hold and gives us all these gifts. But then, like the Corinthians (1 Cor. 11:20-21), he'll say that since God does so much, it doesn't really matter what we do.

Another favorite variation of this trick works the same on both Baptism and the Lord's Supper. Here the sacraments become something you do so that you'll be immune from whatever evil you may get caught in. It's like a smallpox vaccination; you get baptized or go to Communion once in a while and then you can do whatever you want to. Nothing really matters once the sacraments have been "done."

The warning to this trap is the same as it is in the first one. No matter how much he talks about how good and great God's gifts are, the old Adam retains his grip on the action. What God does in the sacraments has to take a back seat to whatever the old Adam wants to get away with.

191

What happens to the sacrament then? It becomes a ticket the old Adam uses to get whatever he wants, a license he shows when he's questioned or in trouble. It is treated like a no-fault insurance policy, picked up at bargain rates every few months or so just in case the old you has an accident.

You can see, then, how both of these traps turn things around so that the old Adam has the action. In the first one, the old Adam figures that he has to help God with God's work. In the second, he figures that God is supposed to help him with old Adam's work. Either way, if you ask, "Who's in charge here?" the old Adam's answer is, "Me! I'm in charge." The old Adam sits in the driver's seat while God is supposed to hitchhike or slump in the back seat like some dim-witted errand boy who doesn't know any better.

How are we going to find our ways between these traps? Take another look at that question, "Who's in charge here?" Who *is* in charge? Who instituted the sacrament of the Lord's Supper? Who said, "This is my body . . . ," "This is my blood . . ." "given and shed for you for the remission of sins"? Who said, "Do this in remembrance of me"?

That's the answer. As long as we try to take over the action, even if it's just trying to find our own way through the traps, we

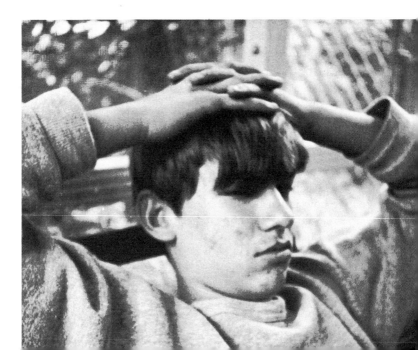

wind up going in circles. The old Adam has us on the merry-go-round again.

But when the Lord's Supper is recognized for what it is, the *Lord's* Supper, his gift to us, all of that changes.

What do you do when you know you're going to receive a great gift? You don't do much of anything, do you? You wait for it, you look forward to the gift, you get ready to receive it. But you certainly don't run around talking about what you've done to deserve the gift, do you? Nor do you set out to try to earn the gift somehow, not if it's really a gift.

And when you're given the gift, what do you do with it? Nobody has to stand over you saying, "Now you have to accept this. You'd better take this gift and look after it." If the gift were poor, cheap, or stupid, somebody might have to say that to you. But if it's a good gift, something you've wanted, you don't have to be told to do anything. You take the gift and open the wrapping as fast as you politely can. And then you thank the person who gave it to you and enjoy the gift you've received.

That's how the Lord's Supper is to be received. It is a sheer, absolute gift in which Christ lays himself open to us, filling us with his gifts.

Because it's a gift, there is nothing you *have to do* to receive it. But because the Lord's Supper is such a great gift, there might be some things you *want to do* just to get ready for it. You might want to fast, for instance, going without food the morning before the sacrament, just to remind yourself that the bread and wine are Christ's gifts. Or you might want to prepare in some other way.

Such preparations "serve a good purpose," as Luther says. But they aren't something we have to do; rather they are some things that we may want to do just because the gift is so great.

The same applies to believing God's promise in the sacrament. If it were something that we had to do "by our own understanding or effort" it would be a chore. Then we would either worry about whether we believe well enough, or end up saying that it doesn't matter.

But when the Lord's Supper is recognized as a gift, then we can look forward to it eagerly. Then we can expect Christ to give us the faith to believe his words, to keep his promise to be present with us. And we can expect him to give us all that goes with his presence. That is believing—expecting the promise, expecting Christ to give you his gifts, counting on him to keep his word.

That's why Christ instituted the Lord's Supper in the first place: to renew you in faith, to break down the barriers that separate you from him and your neighbors, and to open up the future to you. He doesn't require you to believe and then leave you squirming, trying to come up with enough believing. He calls you to faith and then gives it to you, sending his Spirit to speak to you through the word and uphold and uplift you in his sacraments. The Spirit was sent to you in your Baptism, and he will be with you until the last day, to do just that: to give you faith and keep you in it.

That's why the Lord's Supper can also be called the Eucharist, the "thanksgiving." It is Christ's gift to us, a means he uses to assure us that he is with us in our between times. So it is full of joy and thanksgiving, packed full and overflowing with Christ's greatest gift to us: himself. As long as he keeps giving, "nothing will be able to separate us from the love of God in Christ Jesus our Lord" (Rom. 8:39). That's for certain—it is his word.

Chapter 29

Key to the Kingdom

THE OFFICE OF THE KEYS

What is the Office of the Keys?

It is that authority which Christ gave to his church to forgive the sins of those who repent and to declare to those who do not repent that their sins are not forgiven.

What are the words of Christ?

Our Lord Jesus Christ said to his disciples:
"Receive the Holy Spirit. If you forgive the sins of any, they are forgiven; if you retain the sins of any, they are retained" (John 20:23).
"Truly, I say to you, whatever you bind on earth shall be bound in heaven, and whatever you loose on earth shall be loosed in heaven" (Matthew 18:18).

CONFESSION

What is private confession?

Private confession has two parts. First, we make a personal confession of sins to the pastor, and then we receive absolution, which means forgiveness as from God himself. This absolution we should not doubt but firmly believe that thereby our sins are forgiven before God in heaven.

What sins should we confess?

Before God we should confess that we are guilty of all sins, even those which are not known to us, as we do in the Lord's Prayer. But in private confession, as before the pastor, we should confess only those sins which trouble us in heart and mind.

What are such sins?

We can examine our everyday life according to the Ten Commandments—for example, how we act toward father or mother, son or daughter, husband or wife, or toward the people with whom we work and so on. We may ask ourselves whether we have been disobedient or unfaithful, bad tempered or dishonest, or whether we have hurt anyone by word or deed.

How might we confess our sins privately?

We may say that we wish to confess our sins and to receive the absolution in God's name. We may begin by saying, "I, a poor sinner, confess before God that I am guilty of many sins." Then we should name the sins that trouble us. We may close the confession with the words, "I repent of all these sins and pray for mercy. I promise to do better with God's help."

What if we are not troubled by any special sins?

We should not torture ourselves with imaginary sins. If we cannot think of any sins to confess (which would hardly ever happen), we need not name any in particular, but may receive absolution because we have already made a general confession to God.

How may we be assured of forgiveness?

The pastor may pronounce the absolution by saying, "by the authority of our Lord Jesus Christ I forgive you your sins in the name of the Father and of the Son and of the Holy Spirit. Amen." Those who are heavily burdened in conscience the pastor may comfort and encourage with further assurances from God's word.

These two explanations might look strangely out of place in the Catechism. To many people, both the keys and private confession are as Roman Catholic as the Pope and the Vatican.

But the Roman Catholic Church doesn't have a monopoly on these gifts. Christ gave the Office of the Keys to his whole church, and even if you don't recognize the name, it is practiced each Sunday in your congregation.

Private confession isn't practiced so much any more, but it, too, is a part of our heritage. For many centuries, it was a regular part of Lutheran church life.

The keys

The Office of the Keys gets its name from a passage that isn't quoted in the Catechism, but says virtually the same thing as those that are quoted: Matthew 16:19. "I will give you the keys of the kingdom of heaven," Jesus said to Peter and the other disciples, "and whatever you bind on earth shall be bound in heaven and whatever you loose on earth shall be loosed in heaven."

The key to the kingdom is forgiveness—Christ's barrier-breaking, future-opening gift. Just as a key opens a door that has been

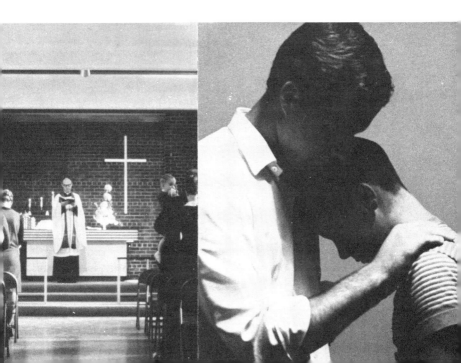

locked shut, Christ's gift of forgiveness breaks down all the barriers the old Adam raises in us, including the old Adam himself.

And, just as a key opens a door so that you can be taken into a house, Christ's gift of forgiveness opens up the future so that he can take you into it. With this gift, Christ opens up all his gifts to you, promising to make you and the whole creation new.

But Jesus went further. He didn't just say, "This is the key," and then leave it hanging on a hook for us to find. He didn't hide it under a mat, either, so we'd have to look for it. He created an office—he appointed janitors—to look after the key, to see to it that the key is used—and used properly. "Receive the Holy Spirit," he said to Peter and all the disciples. "If you forgive the sins of any, they are forgiven; if you retain the sins of any, they are retained" (John 20:23). Through them, he gave the key to his church.

Because Christ has given this key, we can hear his word of forgiveness spoken to us each Sunday. Following the confession of sin at the beginning of each service, the pastor turns to the congregation and says, "Almighty God, our heavenly Father, hath had mercy upon us, and hath given his only Son to die for us, and for his sake forgiveth us all our sins."

As this word is spoken to you, you can be sure God *is* forgiving you all your sin, that he has and always will. Christ himself is turning the key for you as these words are spoken, breaking down your yesterdays and opening up your tomorrows.

Confession

Sometimes, though, the words of absolution spoken on Sunday morning don't strike home the way they should. When they are spoken to the whole congregation, they can leave you wondering if Christ's gift of forgiveness is really meant for you.

In Luther's day, the Roman Catholic Church required private confession, insisting that all people had to confess all their sins before they could receive the Lord's Supper. Confession was, and is, one of the sacraments of the Catholic Church.

During the Reformation, Luther fought some of these requirements regarding private confession. For one thing, there's no basis in Scripture for demanding that a person confess every sin to a pastor or priest before Communion. But more serious, when demands like this are made, confession becomes another one of the old Adam's merry-go-rounds. No matter how much people confess, they can still be left wondering if they've included everything and been completely sincere about it.

But while he fought the requirements in confession, Luther still insisted that it is a precious gift. He took away the demand to confess everything, saying that "we should confess only those sins which trouble us in heart and mind." And he stopped considering it a sacrament because it doesn't have a physical sign or element, like the water of Baptism and the bread and wine of the Lord's Supper. But he strongly urged all who consider themselves Christians to go to private confession and hear the absolution spoken directly to them.

It is hearing the words of the absolution spoken directly and personally to each of us that makes private confession so powerful and helpful.

Confessing your sins privately with your pastor gives you a chance to get anything that is bothering you off your chest, to talk it over with someone you can trust. Your pastor's job isn't to condemn you for your sin, or to lecture you about how worthless you have been. Rather, your pastor's job is to help you discover the old Adam's tricks and traps, to hear you as you confess, and to tell you how God has promised to help you do better.

This alone makes confession a great gift. Oftentimes, just being able to talk over what you're ashamed of or afraid of with someone you can trust will lighten your load.

But there's even more. As the pastor speaks the words of the absolution to you directly, in person, God himself is breaking down your barriers and opening up the future to you. "By the authority of our Lord Jesus Christ I forgive you all your sins in the name of the Father and of the Son and of the Holy Spirit," the pastor can say.

The practice of private confession was discontinued among Lutherans for many different reasons. But the old Adam is the one who really stole it, hiding it from us. Though not required, with the Word and the sacraments confession is a means God uses to give us the certainty of faith as we look forward to the dawning of his new day.

Chapter 30

Conversation and Consolation

"We shall now return to the Gospel, which offers counsel and help against sin in more than one way, for God is surpassingly rich in his grace: First, through the spoken word, by which the forgiveness of sin (the peculiar function of the Gospel) is preached to the whole world; second, through Baptism; third, through the holy Sacrament of the Altar; fourth, through the power of the keys; and finally, through the mutual conversation and consolation of the brethren. Matthew 18:20, 'Where two or three are gathered,' etc."

Smalcald Articles   Part III, Article IV

God's grace comes to us in one other way that is often over-looked. Sometimes it is considered too common or natural to be any of God's concern. Oftentimes it goes by unnoticed, as one of those things that just happens.

Yet you've probably seen it in operation, and drawn strength and encouragement from it. In fact, it's probably one of the most important things that has happened for you in your congregation.

Luther called it "the mutual conversation and consolation of the brethren." It is the friendship or fellowship that you give and receive as you reach out to and share your gifts with other people in your congregation and community.

Maybe that does seem too common or natural to be any of God's concern. Your conversations with others from your church may not always be particularly sanctified. And the gifts you share with one another may seem small and insignificant. You might not even consider them gifts.

But as Luther says in that statement from the Smalcald Articles printed at the beginning of this unit, "mutual conversation and consolation" not only *can be* but *is* a means God uses to keep us in his grace.

Your priesthood

The clues to how this "mutual conversation and consolation" becomes an avenue of God's grace are in the Third Article of the Creed and the Sacrament of Baptism.

The Spirit loves company, you remember. As he goes to work in the Word and the sacraments to give us the certainty of faith, the Spirit is always gathering us together with other people—whether in twos and threes, tens and twelves, or hundreds and thousands. The company of others in your congregations isn't an accident. As a member of the church, you are part of the "communion of saints," the community of people put together by the Spirit.

But that's not all the Spirit does. In Baptism, as God declares his decision about us and makes us his own, the Spirit makes each one of us his priests or pastors. He calls out the new you in us so that we can speak the word with the people he has gathered; so that we can comfort and help one another along the way.

That may sound like a strange way to put it. Only one person, or at most a few, is regularly called "pastor" in your congregation. But God is far too generous to leave you with just one pastor, or even a dozen. He surrounds you with pastors, making every baptized person one of them.

Your pastor, the one who preaches on Sunday, was elected by your congregation to hold a special office. In that office, your pastor's calling is to see to it that the word is properly preached and the sacraments rightly administered.

But your pastor doesn't replace you. Though you might never enter a pulpit, baptize a child, or give the Lord's Supper, as one of God's people you are a pastor, too. No matter where you go, no matter what kind of job you wind up doing for a living, you can speak the word of God to others. You can comfort and console, help and encourage others in your congregation. Others can do the same for you. With them, you are a part of what Luther called "the priesthood of all believers."

One of the best examples of how this ministry happens takes place when someone from your church dies. Then people from your congregation gather around the family to comfort them, to say the word of love and hope, to help out in many different ways. It's not always easy, but in this way grieving families are strengthened and upheld in difficult times. That is "the mutual conversation and consolation of the brethren"—the kind of help the Spirit gives us as he gathers us together with others.

But it doesn't only happen at a time of death. It goes on all your life long. The comments you've made and the questions you asked as you've studied the Catechism, for instance, may have helped others gain a deeper understanding. Getting together to have a program and some fun at church youth groups may have encouraged you or opened the door to some new friends.

It's this giving and taking, this talking and listening, that the Spirit uses to help each of us. It is a ministry that we have to one another in our churches.

Your gifts

This ministry we have together doesn't only happen in conversation. As Paul describes the church in Romans 12 and 1 Corinthians 12-14, he speaks of a whole variety of gifts the Spirit gives us so that we can serve in other ways, too.

The Holy Spirit doesn't have an assembly line that turns out everyone the same. He makes us all different, giving each of us particular gifts. Some of the gifts Paul mentions are preaching, service, teaching, encouraging, contributing, giving aid, acting mercifully, helping, healing, and even organizing meetings. Along with these gifts are others like prophecy and speaking in tongues.

Having given us our gifts the Spirit takes us and binds us together in our congregations to pool these gifts. He unites us as his people, making us a community, so that we can each give from our strengths to make good each other's weaknesses. We are made one body, as Paul says, the body of Christ. Just as hands, feet, arms, and legs serve different purposes for the same person, we have different gifts and functions but we are united as one in Christ.

The purpose of our gifts isn't to serve ourselves though. As the Spirit gives us the word and the gifts that go with it, he turns us both inward and outward—in towards the people we belong with in the church, and out towards all who have not yet heard the word or been grasped by it. That's the church's purpose: to speak the word to all who have ears to hear, to give the gifts we share to any and all who need them.

"He unites us as his people, making us a community."

The old Adam turns up his nose at these gifts just as he turns up his nose at everything God gives. "The mutual conversation and consolation of the brethren," as the old Adam sees it, is just so much talk—people getting together in the church to visit as they do everywhere else. It's "just fellowship"—something you can do anywhere; or it's all fellowship, that's all the church has to offer.

The old Adam does the same thing to the Spirit's gifts. In his eyes, they are just "talents," some sort of special abilities you're born with so that you can impress people or make lots of money. Or else the old Adam puts on some religion again and claims that

your gifts give you a corner on God's market, insisting that you must be the finest Christian around.

Either way, as the old Adam takes them, God's gifts are just common, ordinary, natural things to be used in the ordinary way—to take care of yourself.

That's not how God sees these gifts. He never turns up his nose at what's common, ordinary, and natural. He's the one who made all things, all that's great and all that's common, all that's beautiful and all that's ordinary. He's the one who was born in an ordinary stable to become a person like us. He's the one who died a terrifying natural death and was put away in an ordinary grave. He's the one who raised Jesus from the dead; the one who sends his Spirit to speak to us in ordinary words, to make us his, to assure us and reassure us that we belong to him by using natural things as common as water, bread, and wine.

It is this God, the God who lays himself open to us in Christ Jesus, who has decided to be your God. That's his decision. That's his promise—that he is taking you as you are, with all that's great and all that's common about you, with all that's beautiful and all that's ordinary about you, to make you new, one of his very own.

He's going to make you what Adam and Eve were made to be in the first place. He's going to make you a believer, one who will take him at his word just because it is his word. He's going to make you a lover who will give your gifts to your neighbors just because they're neighbors. He's going to make you a lover who cares for the earth—for all that's common, ordinary and natural—just because it's his creation.

But that's not all. As he makes you new, God's going to make his whole creation new, bringing in the new heavens and the new earth. Then the old Adam, death, and the devil will be gone, washed up once and for all. Then God will dwell with us, as loving fathers and mothers live with their children.

In the meantime, God gives us all that we need: his Word, the sacraments, and the company of others. They are his gifts, given in the Spirit to make us new each day, to hold and keep us until the new day comes. It's for certain. It's his promise. He's decided. He keeps his Word.

Daily Prayers

GRACE AT TABLE

When children and the whole household gather at thy table, they should reverently fold their hands and say:
"The eyes of all look to thee, O Lord,
and thou givest them their food in due season.
Thou openest thy hand; thou satisfiest the desire
of every living thing."

(It is to be observed that "satisfying the desire of every living thing" means that all creatures receive enough to eat to make them joyful and of good cheer. Greed and anxiety about food prevent such satisfaction.)

Then the Lord's Prayer should be said, and afterwards this prayer:
"Lord God, heavenly Father, bless us, and these thy gifts,
which of thy bountiful goodness thou hast bestowed on us,
through Jesus Christ our Lord. Amen."

THANKSGIVING AFTER EATING

After eating, likewise, they should fold their hands reverently and say:
"O give thanks to the Lord, for he is good;
for his steadfast love endures forever.
He gives to the beasts their food,
and to the young ravens which cry.
His delight is not in the strength of the horse,
nor his pleasure in the legs of a man;
but the Lord takes pleasure in those who fear him,
in those who hope in his steadfast love."

Then the Lord's Prayer should be said, and afterwards this prayer:
"We give thee thanks, Lord God, our Father,
for all thy benefits, through Jesus Christ our Lord,
who lives and reigns forever. Amen."

MORNING AND EVENING PRAYERS

In the morning, when you rise, make the sign of the cross and say, "In the name of God, the Father, the Son, and the Holy Spirit. Amen."

Then, kneeling or standing, say the Apostles' Creed and the Lord's Prayer. Then you may say this prayer:

"I give thee thanks, heavenly Father,
through thy dear Son Jesus Christ,
that thou hast protected me through the night
from all harm and danger. I beseech thee to keep me
this day, too, from all sin and evil,
that in all my thoughts, words, and deeds
I may please thee. Into thy hands I commend my body
and soul and all that is mine.
Let thy holy angel have charge of me,
that the wicked one may have no power over me. Amen."

After singing a hymn (possibly a hymn on the Ten Commandments) or whatever your devotion may suggest, you should go to your work joyfully.

In the evening, when you retire, make the sign of the cross and say, "In the name of God, the Father, the Son, and the Holy Spirit. Amen."

Then, kneeling or standing, say the Apostles' Creed and the Lord's Prayer. Then you may say this prayer:

"I give thee thanks, heavenly Father,
through thy dear Son Jesus Christ,
that thou hast this day graciously protected me.
I beseech thee to forgive all my sin
and the wrong which I have done. Graciously protect me
during the coming night. Into thy hands I commend
my body and soul and all that is mine.
Let thy holy angels have charge of me,
that the wicked one may have no power over me. Amen."

Then quickly lie down and sleep in peace.

These prayers were originally included
in Luther's Small Catechism.

208